THEIR PROMISED LAND

ALSO BY IAN BURUMA

Theater of Cruelty: Art, Film, and the Shadows of War

Year Zero: A History of 1945

Taming the Gods:
Religion and Democracy on Three Continents

The China Lover: A Novel

Murder in Amsterdam: Liberal Europe, Islam,
and the Limits of Tolerance

Conversations with John Schlesinger

Occidentalism: The West in the Eyes of Its Enemies

Inventing Japan: 1853–1964

Bad Elements: Chinese Rebels from Los Angeles to Beijing

The Wages of Guilt: Memories of War in Germany and Japan

Anglomania: A European Love Affair

The Missionary and the Libertine: Love and War in East and West

Playing the Game

Behind the Mask: On Sexual Demons, Sacred Mothers, Transvestites,
Gangsters, Drifters and Other Japanese Cultural Heroes

The Japanese Tattoo (text by Donald Richie,
photographs by Ian Buruma)

IAN BURUMA

THEIR PROMISED LAND

My Grandparents in Love and War

First published in the United States of America in 2016 by
The Penguin Press, a member of Penguin Group (USA) LLC.

First published in hardback and trade paperback in
Great Britain in 2016 by Atlantic Books,
an imprint of Atlantic Books Ltd.

1 2 3 4 5 6 7 8 9

A CIP catalogue record for this book is available from
the British Library.

Hardback ISBN: 978-1-84887-938-6
Trade Paperback ISBN: 978-1-84887-940-9
E-book ISBN: 978-1-78239-541-6
Paperback ISBN: 978-1-84887-941-6

Printed in Sweden by ScandBook AB
Atlantic Books
An Imprint of Atlantic Books Ltd
Ormond House
26–27 Boswell Street
London
WC1N 3JZ

www.atlantic-books.co.uk

For Isabel and Josephine

CONTENTS

———·———

THEIR
PROMISED
LAND

DON'T LIKE THE NAME

———·——

Asked whether he believed in happy marriage,
Philip Roth replied: "Yes, and some people play the
violin like Isaac Stern. But it's rare."

—Claudia Roth Pierpont,
Roth Unbound: A Writer and His Books

When I think of my maternal grandparents, I think of Christmas. Since they both lived into the 1980s, I can think of many other things too. But Christmas at St. Mary Woodlands House, the large vicarage in Berkshire where they lived next to Woodlands St. Mary's, a mid-Victorian Gothic church, now no longer in use, will always be my childhood idyll.

Age in these memories is rather indistinct. Anything between six and fourteen, I suppose. Roughly between 1958 and 1966. Between grey Marks and Spencer shorts and my powderblue Beatles hat.

Nothing could ever match the thrill of arriving late at night, exhausted and a little sick from spending much of the day in our family car thick with my mother's cigarette smoke, having started early that morning in The Hague, crossing the choppy North Sea on a Belgian ferryboat smelling of petrol fumes and vomit (the British Rhine Army going home), waiting for hours in the customs shed at Dover, crawling endlessly along one-lane country roads, taking in the familiar English winter odours of soot and bonfire smoke, and then finally pulling into the gravelled drive of St. Mary Woodlands, to be greeted with the jovial laughter of my grandfather, "Grandpop," wearing a green tweed jacket and smoking a pipe.

The two-storey house with its large windows and elephant-grey stucco walls was not grand, even though my memory has greatly expanded its size as though it were one of the great English country houses. It was not. But it was spacious. And it gave off a sense of solid Victorian comfort. A lawn, about the size of two football fields, at the rear of the house, flanked by broad flowerbeds tended by my grandmother, backed into a line of high oak trees, home to hundreds of cawing rooks, looking out to what is now the M4 motorway.

The lawn was used in summer for games of croquet and village fêtes. Ladies in hats inspected the wooden tables laden with prize fruits, vegetables, and homemade cakes. There were coconut shies, a tombola, and lucky dips. The vicar of St. Mary's mingled with surgeons, retired colonels, assorted family members, and the odd local aristocrat, such as Lady S., who was cheerfully drunk before lunch, and usually accompanied by a formidable lady in tweeds, known to us as "Major C."

Christmas at St. Mary Woodlands,
my sister and me

Sherry was served on the terrace. High tea came with cakes, scones, chocolate biscuits, and cucumber sandwiches. These domestic scenes were always bathed in sunshine, of course, followed by the long shadows and golden light of early summer evenings.

Just so, in my mind's eye, the lawn never failed to be buried under a thick blanket of snow at Christmas.

After piling out of my father's car, we would enter the house through the kitchen, where Laura, the beloved family

cook, hovered over the stove, a cigarette dangling from the corner of her mouth on the verge of dripping ash onto a freshly
roasted lamb.

There were other "char ladies" who loom large in my childhood memories, such as the toothless Mrs. Tuttle, the pale and
birdlike Mrs. Dobson, and an enormously stout lady with a
neighing laugh, named Mrs. Mackerell, with whose husband,
"Old Butt," my grandfather would repair once a year to a local
pub for his Christmas drink.

To the side of the kitchen was Laura's room, a dark, messy
space with a strong whiff of sweat, dog, and unwashed stockings. This was where the only television set in the house was in-
stalled. TV was not really approved of by my grandparents,
hence perhaps its banishment to the house's least salubrious
corner. I spent many happy hours there, alone or sometimes
with Laura, watching English comedy shows in black and white
(Frankie Howerd and Sidney James) and American westerns
(*The Lone Ranger* and *Gunsmoke*). No one else watched television much. An exception was made when a member of the family was on the TV. My aunt Susan played Samuel Pepys's wife in
a series based on his diaries; my uncle John, before becoming a
famous film director, made documentaries for the BBC about
fine English cheeses, World War II generals, art school students, and Georges Simenon speaking about his sexual con-
quests through a haze of tobacco smoke. John also had a brief
career as an actor. I remember seeing him in Laura's room as a
minstrel pretending to play the mandolin while singing a song
to Roger Moore in an episode of *Ivanhoe*.

A narrow passage led from the kitchen to the main hall,

My grandmother and me in 1953

where a wide and elegant staircase climbed to the bedrooms on the first floor. From early December onward the walls along the stairs were covered up to the ceiling in Christmas cards, hundreds and hundreds of them, like leaves of ivy on a garden wall. Making sure to send Christmas cards to everyone she knew, or who might possibly be offended if they didn't get one, was an annual source of neurotic obsession for my grandmother, or "Granny," who would be mortified to receive a card from anyone she might possibly have overlooked.

It was not just the Christmas cards that spoke of a certain air of excess. Everything about Christmas seemed a trifle over-done, certainly more lavish than anything we were used to at home in Holland—the mistletoe, the ubiquitous holly, the candles, and especially, in the large drawing room looking out onto the garden, the Christmas tree, whose opulence, like so much else, might be slightly magnified by memory, but not much. Dripping with gold and silver baubles, festooned with streams of glittery trimmings, angels dangling from pretty little candlesticks, the tree was topped by a shining angel stretching her arms all the way to the high ceiling. This totem of pagan abundance, looking over a small mountain range of beautifully wrapped presents at its base, was not really vulgar—Granny had excellent taste. It was just very, very big.

The impression was clear: here was a family that was serious about Christmas.

Christmas Day, for my two sisters and me, began as early as four or five o'clock in the morning, when we could no longer contain ourselves and would fall upon the Christmas stockings, seemingly made for giants, bulging with nuts, chocolates, fruits, and a panoply of presents. Gifts that were too bulky to be stuffed into these huge cotton sausages were tied to them with string: an illustrated edition of Kipling's *Jungle Book*, a much-wished-for toy Colt revolver, a set of paints and brushes, a plastic model of a Lancaster bomber, and much more that I have forgotten. Family friends who stayed as guests and received equally bountiful stockings assumed that this was the extent of the Christmas presents, slightly baffled why this seasonal ritual was dealt with so early in the day. Little did they know.

After a cup of tea and biscuits taken in bed, a cooked breakfast was waiting for us on warm silver domed platters laid out on the mahogany sideboard in the downstairs dining room.

There were sausages and tomatoes, devilled kidneys, plump brown kippers glistening in butter, scrambled, poached, or boiled eggs freshly hatched in the chicken coop next to the gardener's cottage, and various kinds of toast with an assortment of homemade jams. This was just the beginning of a daylong feast of Edwardian gluttony, interrupted only by a brisk walk in the morning on the snowy top of Inkpen Beacon, marked by an old wooden gibbet where murderers used to be hanged. Then came the opening of presents after lunch, and a languid hour or two after tea of listening to classical music records presented to one another by the adults.

There was always music at St. Mary Woodlands. Classical music was a kind of family cult, and deep knowledge about opera, especially Wagner's operas, as well as the music of Brahms, Mozart, and Beethoven, was almost a requirement. As was playing an instrument with some degree of skill. Granny had been a very fine violinist. Aunt Hilary had played the violin as a professional. And my mother, Wendy, was a keen amateur cellist. Uncle John had played the piano, but switched as a teenager, much to the dismay of his parents, to performing conjuring tricks. Hilary's twin brother, Uncle Roger, once played the French horn. He probably knew more about music than anyone else—the classics, that is, modern music being dismissed as "plonkety-plonk," and pop music as rubbish.

My father's taste ran to jazz, which was tolerated in moderation, since he had after all married my mother, who shared some of his passions, but this was sometimes the subject of good-natured mockery. Noël Coward, revered by my grandfather—aside from Brahms, whose music never failed to bring a tear to his eyes—was one thing, Duke Ellington quite another. My own fondness as a teenager for Cliff Richard was, however, disapproved of. I could have my wished-for Cliff Richard records, but had to listen to *The Young Ones* or *Expresso Bongo* with the sound turned right down, my ears glued to the mono loudspeaker under the grand piano when no one else was around. Uncle John, who bought me my first Cliff Richard LPs, also included a record of Nat King Cole, whose songs were considered more elevating. I outgrew Cliff Richard but never really developed a taste for Nat King Cole.

Christmas lunch was a succession of traditional dishes, beautifully cooked by Laura: turkey filled with stuffing, sausages, bread sauce, and so on, followed by a rich plum pudding carried into the darkened dining room with much pomp by Laura, whose annual tear would drop into the flaming brandy.

In the old days, before World War II, when the family lived in London, my grandparents would dress up every night for dinner, while their children were confined to the nursery. Standards had been relaxed since then. And the family was no longer required to jump to attention during the monarch's Christmas speech either.

Grandpop sat at the head of the table, an absurd paper hat from a Christmas cracker wrapped around his bald head and a pipe firmly lodged between his nicotine-stained teeth. He had the appearance of a friendly frog, his round face creased with laughter. He was a paediatrician, and his main prescription for a healthy life was the combination of fresh air and alcohol. When we were very small, he would offer us a brandy cork to sniff. When I was about fourteen I was given the choice between beer and cider to drink at lunch. My choice of cider did not entirely please him, since beer was considered a more manly drink. When the Christmas weather was especially severe, he would smack his lips and announce that he would spend the night outside on the lawn. Always on cue, my grandmother would protest (which was the whole point), and after a ritual palaver the plan was quietly abandoned.

My mother's youngest sibling was Aunt Susan, the most bohemian among the immediate family members; she once insisted on travelling across Spain barefoot, leaving her with a painful skin disease. Susan was having some success as an actress, not just on television, but as a member of the Royal Shakespeare Company (she played Nerissa in a famous Stratford production with Peter O'Toole as Shylock). We adored her. Other members of the family sitting around the Christmas table included Gabriel, Uncle Roger's first wife, and their son, Paul. The men in my mother's family were all short, stocky, and prematurely bald, and the women were even shorter and had thick wavy dark brown hair, except for Aunt Susan, who was fair, and Granny, whose perfectly coiffed hair was set in waves of salt and pepper.

Uncle John often invited a "chum" down for Christmas, who would share his bedroom. When I was very young, I never quite understood why these nice young men didn't want to marry my aunt Susan. After all, they usually shared an interest in "the stage."

The family conversation might best be described as a kind of creative chaos. The main thing was to be heard in the cacophony of stories and inside jokes. You had to be quick if you were to be noticed. Sharp wit and the skill to tell a good story were essential, preferably at the top of your voice. The worst possible sin was to be a bore. Faces under the coloured paper hats grew steadily ruddier as candles flickered in the silver candelabra and the contents of the Christmas crackers sprawled across the table amid the walnuts, the dried fruits, and the crystal glasses. Opera performances around Europe were recalled. Family anecdotes retold. John and Roger giggled like schoolboys. And Granny and Grandpop sat back and surveyed the scene with patriarchal and matriarchal pride.

No wonder these occasions could strike an outsider as a trifle overpowering. It was hard to get a word in. We were a tight-knit clan. And yet the family was far from closed to outsiders. On the contrary, my grandparents had a quasi-Oriental concept of hospitality. They took pride in the number of guests they welcomed at St. Mary Woodlands. It was a sign of their generosity. Rather like those Christmas cards in the hall, friends were proof of the family's worth, even perhaps of its acceptance.

I cannot say I felt overpowered. But coming as my sisters and I were from a relatively provincial Dutch town, the glamour of family Christmas in England made our lives seem rather drab in comparison. If acceptance was an issue, it was about my place in the family, and the culture it represented. This was not a straightforward matter. Even the tightest-knit clans consist of concentric circles. At the centre, holding it all together, were the grandparents, Granny and Grandpop, Bernard and Winifred ("Bun" and "Win"), around whom everything revolved. The following circles were made up of the next generations. But the family extended further, to circles of great-uncles and -aunts, cousins, and nephews and nieces, and then there were even more distant relatives, some of them refugees from twentieth-century catastrophes, and an adopted family of twelve Jewish children whom my grandparents had helped to escape from Hitler's Berlin.

I grew up in the warm embrace of the inner circle, trying to come up to the image I had of my grandparents, their grandeur in my eyes, St. Mary Woodlands.

An idyll is usually associated with a pastoral scene, a childhood Garden of Eden, a place to which there can be no return. Mine was set in a very English countryside. Everything about St. Mary Woodlands—the fêtes, the pony rides in summertime, the village cricket, and, above all, Christmas—seemed very, very English. And indeed, the superiority of Englishness, to my grandparents, was never in doubt. They were far too well travelled and cosmopolitan to look down on foreigners, let alone to exclude them. They were not like the guest at a local Sunday-morning drinks party, who replied to my mother's casual remark, made in a flagging attempt at small talk, that our car in the drive was the only one with foreign number plates, that this was "nothing to be proud of." On the contrary, English superiority would more often be expressed by being especially polite to foreigners, while being careful not to seem patronizing.

And yet my sisters and I were made aware from a very early age that there was something faintly amusing about our foreign background, about the way we spoke an incomprehensible guttural language, or "Double Dutch," as the family would call it. John and his chums delighted in doing imitations of Queen

Juliana's admittedly comical accent in her efforts to speak English.

And so, to live up to the idyll of St. Mary Woodlands, I became something far more laughable than being foreign; I became a little Anglophile, an aspiration my grandparents, perhaps feeling secretly flattered, were happy to indulge: cricket bats and checked Viyella shirts for Christmas, regimental ties and blue blazers for my birthdays. My pocket money was spent on comics, like *Eagle* or *Beano*, featuring English public schoolboy heroes winning football games, and blond, square-jawed RAF aces downing Messerschmitts.

As with the Cliff Richard records, this too I outgrew in time. But perhaps never entirely. Like a memory of Eden, the aura of St. Mary Woodlands will never quite fade away. The superior Englishness represented by my grandparents will remain unattainable, and yet it lingers, as a kind of distant goal, or perhaps just a form of nostalgia.

I once introduced an American friend to my grandparents, years after they had moved from St. Mary Woodlands to a more manageable cottage nearby. It must have been sometime in the late 1970s; we had been to see a new punk rock band in London the night before. My friend, Jim, said that my grandparents were the most English people he had ever met. Their home, he said, was like something out of Agatha Christie.

And yet the Englishness of my grandparents was not as clear-cut as it seemed. For they too aspired to a kind of idyll. They also lived up to an ideal. Apart from my grandfather's mother, Estella

Ellinger, who was born in Manchester, my great-grandparents all came from Germany. As did Estella's father, Alexander Ellinger. Her mother, Mathilda van Oven, was born in Holland. They were all German Jews. Which is to say that my grandparents, Bernard Schlesinger and Win Regensburg, were English in the way their German Jewish ancestors were German, and that was, if such a thing were possible, more so, or at least more self-consciously so, than the "natives."

This was partly a matter of class. Already solidly middle-class in Germany, my family did even better in England, where at least one of my two maternal great-grandfathers made a fortune as a stockbroker in the City of London. It is the old immigrant story, assimilation as the sign of higher education and prosperity. Jews like my grandparents, in Germany, France, Holland, or Hungary, wanted to shed their minority status, as though it were an unsightly scar. Marks of difference—language, customs, dress, even religion, at least of the Orthodox kind—had been discarded. They wished to be accepted as something they genuinely were: loyal citizens steeped, often more so than the Gentiles themselves, in the cultures they had made their own. If anything, there was an overeagerness to do well, to speak German, French, or English more correctly, more beautifully than the Gentiles, to be more deeply versed in the literature or the music—and, of course, have finer Christmas trees.

German Jews in particular are still ridiculed by Jews with Eastern European roots for their stiff manners and highfalutin ways. The typical *Yekke*, as he is called in Israel, punctilious, pedantic, quick to disapprove, the type of immigrant who insists on dressing in a three-piece suit under the palm trees of the Holy Land, is a figure of fun, as well as being rather despised. It was typical *Yekkes* who thought the Nazis would never touch *them*, because they had fought in the Great War and had the medals to prove it. This type of tragic illusion was less the object of pity than of scorn.

That *Yekkes* often treated poorer, less assimilated Jews with snobbish disdain, as unwelcome riff-raff who would give decent civilized Jews a bad name, is beyond doubt. My grandparents were not entirely immune to this type of snobbery. The Israeli philosopher Moshe Halbertal, an Orthodox Jew born in Uruguay, once pointed out to me the important distinction between assimilated and "closeted" Jews. He disapproved of the latter. I would say my grandparents were more assimilated than closeted, although my grandmother at times had at least one leg behind the closet door.

They never converted to Christianity, at any rate, and never denied their Jewish background. My grandfather grew up in an Orthodox household; his father—a great lover of Richard Wagner's music, by the way—had insisted on that. But there was not a trace of his religious upbringing left by the time I knew him (except possibly a hint of grumpiness on Christmas morning). Jewishness was often a topic of conversation in the family. I have no idea where the family code word "forty-five," meaning Jewish, came from or when it was first used. But my grandmother in particular was always keen to find out whether a new friend or acquaintance was "forty-five." Some people (all my close relations) looked distinctly "forty-five," and some didn't. But it was a neutral term, which bestowed no special merit, or indeed demerit, to the person under scrutiny.

To be Jewish, then, was not a source of shame. My grandparents just didn't want to make a fuss about it, lest others might be tempted to do so. They were born in England, were educated in the usual manner of the English upper middle class: public school, in his case, and Oxford and Cambridge. They were British and had the perfect right to insist on it, and yet their sense of belonging was never simply to be taken for granted.

Their loyalty to Britain and its institutions was perhaps extreme, but it partly came from gratitude. The society in which they were born and bred did not turn on them, as Germany had done on its most loyal Jewish citizens. When there were instances of anti-Jewish prejudice, Bernard and Win, as I shall call them from now on, were usually too proud to show that it bothered them. The retired colonel in the local village, who was heard to mutter when my grandparents moved there, "Don't like the name, don't like the money," was a figure of fun in the family, his words quoted as a kind of running gag at the Christmas table. And so Bernard volunteered for army service every time there was a crisis, all the way up to the Cuban missiles, when he was already in his sixties and had to be politely informed that his services to queen and country were no longer really required.

It is easy to curl one's lip from the relative safety of a different age at their sense of gratitude. Grateful for what? Now their kind of melting into the Gentile world might be considered a form of denial, even cowardice. Why didn't they insist on their true "identity" as Jews? But I refuse to see their lives in that light. Who is to say what anyone's true identity is anyway? If they made a conscious choice, it was to move away from the narrow circle of their parents, the genteel Hampstead world of German Jewish immigrants, well-off, cultivated, but largely confined to their own kind. Bernard and Win were not immigrants and felt no need to seek the security of an émigré milieu. And yet certain aspects of the German Jewish background stuck with them: the worship of classical music, my grandmother's anxiety always to be at her best, never to stick out, to avoid embarrassment at all costs, the exaggerated patriotism, and the almost fetishistic love of family, as a haven of safety.

Inside this haven, the two of them had built an impregnable fortress of their own. More than anything else, including their country, or even their own children, they adored each other. It was there, in their family of two, that they really felt safe. There is something idyllic about such rare unions, romantic and unassailable. When they died, Bernard in 1984 and Win in 1986, the family really disintegrated with them. Once they were gone, the centre did not hold.

Two of their children, my mother, who died of cancer at the age of forty-three, and Susan, who killed herself at the age of thirty, went long before them. John, mute after several strokes, died in Palm Springs, California, in 2003. Roger followed a few years later. Only Hilary is still alive, a member of the Opus Dei, after having converted to Roman Catholicism many years ago.

I sometimes go on a sentimental journey to St. Mary Woodlands. But apart from the familiar landscape, nothing of my idyll remains. The main house looks oddly cramped and is painted in a different colour, the garden looks nothing like the way it did before, and the gardener's cottage is now a separate and no doubt expensive country home. Then there is the distant roar of traffic on the M4. I am sure it is still a lovely place for someone. But an idyll can exist only in memory.

The lives of most people, unless they were very famous, slip away into oblivion when those who still remember them die in their turn. These days few people even leave a record of their existence; whatever is there in digital form will disappear soon. E-mails are not written to last.

But Bernard and Win did leave a record, not because they wished to be immortal or even wanted others to see it, but simply because they couldn't bear the thought of throwing it away. In the barn of John's country house in Sussex was a stack of steel boxes filled with mouse droppings and hundreds of letters, the first of which was written in 1915, when Bernard was still at boarding school and Win was studying music in London. The last ones were written in the 1970s.

Most of them are love letters, written from the trenches in France in World War I, from Oxford and Cambridge in the 1920s, from Germany in the 1930s, from a variety of places in

World War II. Often, especially when Bernard was away for three years in India as an army doctor during the war, they wrote every day, knowing the letters would take weeks, and sometimes months, to reach the other side. Even though some are missing, I don't think that even one letter was ever consciously thrown away. They express their most intimate thoughts and emotions which were never supposed to be read by anyone else. (When her father died, Win burnt all his letters, because she believed that it would be rude to read a person's private correspondence.) They may well have been alarmed at the thought that theirs would be read one day by their grandson, who is considerably older now than they were when the bulk of the letters were written, much less by a larger audience.

None of us have identical memories of people. We all make up stories about those we love, or hate, just as we do about ourselves. The story about Bernard and Win that I have pieced together from their letters may not have been the story chosen by others who knew them, let alone by themselves. Some might, for instance, have put more emphasis on their generosity, not just in material terms, supporting people with money, or giving thoughtful presents. Their generosity of spirit was at least as remarkable.

One story that stands out for me, as an example, is beyond the scope of this book, which ends in 1945, but is still intimately linked to their narrative as I have chosen to present it. After all their talk in wartime letters of the hateful Germans, whose targets of mass killing would, if they had been able to reach them, have included Bernard and Win and all their children, after all the news of murdered relatives, of the mounds of corpses at Bergen-Belsen, and the gas chambers of Auschwitz, after all that, they contacted a German POW camp near Newbury in 1946 to invite two of Hitler's former soldiers to spend Christmas at their family home in Kintbury.

It was, in my aunt Hilary's recollection, a somewhat stilted occasion. How could it have been otherwise? Too much had to be left unspoken. The immediate past was still mined with explosives, however innocent these particular Germans might have been of one of history's darkest crimes. It was too soon for a Jewish family to celebrate Christmas with German soldiers.

But the Germans never forgot this gesture of kindness. For them it restored a sense of humanity that had been all but destroyed in the last decade. I like to think that Bernard and Win reached out to these men in the same spirit with which they rescued the twelve Jewish children. They did it out of common decency. I say common, but in fact, of course, it was highly uncommon.

There is much of this spirit in the letters. But decency is not the same thing as love, which is the main subject of the correspondence. Expressions of love, except in good poetry, when they are transformed into art, can be cloying. In fact, the love between Bernard and Win is not the main subject of this book either. Instead, I have selected passages that express how they saw themselves in relation to the world they lived in. What interested me were the stories they told each other and themselves about who they were.

Questions of class, culture, and nationality can be addressed in a scholarly way, with statistics and sociological theory. But this was of no interest to me. I wanted to find out how two people very close to me dealt with these questions themselves. They are questions I have asked myself in pretty much every book I have written. The reason is autobiographical. Growing up with more than one culture, with parents of different nationalities and religious backgrounds (I leave race and ethnicity aside), forces one to think about one's place in the world. It is the fate of all people who feel for one reason or another that they are in a minority. If you are in the majority, you can afford to swim along with the mainstream without giving it too much thought. But a Jew in a society of mostly Gentiles, a Muslim in Europe, a black in a predominantly white country, or a homosexual, especially in places where love of your own sex is unaccepted, is forced to consider his or her place more deeply, to make up his or her own story.

This implies choice. Some of us have more freedom to choose our own identities than others, depending on time, place, and social position. I had more freedom than my grandparents. They had more freedom than people from a less privileged background, or Jews faced with more anti-Semitism.

Bernard and Win wrote to one another about their place in the world as insiders who were outsiders too, a perspective that also marks the films of their son John: *Billy Liar, Midnight Cowboy, Sunday Bloody Sunday, An Englishman Abroad*. By using their own words, I have contrived to produce a kind of novel in letters, with myself as a kind of Greek chorus. What emerged might not be how they would have liked to see themselves. Their portraits inevitably reflect my own preoccupations, so it should be read as a type of memoir as well. And always, in the background, like a classical score, there is the music that accompanied the lives of two very British Jews, whose favourite piece was composed by Richard Wagner as a private tribute to his wife and children: the *Siegfried Idyll*. It was first performed in 1870, on Christmas Day.

One

FIRST LOVE

——·——

April 25, 1915:

Dear Winnie,

I hope you won't get bored with this effusion of
correspondence. But, no,—I don't see why I should
apologize as you are one up on me & this in the shape
of a letter. Moreover it is only polite to answer a letter
from a lady. So "as you were" & cross all this first lot
out. This brings me back to the beginning, doesn't it
& nothing said but a whole page used? That is "comme
il est fait" as they say in Germany.

So begins the first letter in my possession sent by Bernard
to Winnie, as he still called her then. It can't have been the first
one he ever wrote. In a letter written in 1919, he reminds her
of her first letters to him, signed "Winifred Regensburg."

Win in Hampstead

Winifred was a name she loathed with a passion, hence the change to Winnie, or later to Win, or sometimes Wincie, anything but Winifred.

The facetious tone is that of the jokey schoolboy that Bernard would adopt on occasion for the rest of his life. "Ooooh, Doctor!" the cleaning ladies would squeal as he rolled the empty beer bottles along the corridor to the kitchen at St. Mary Woodlands when he was well into his seventies. He was nineteen years old when he wrote this letter. Win was a year younger.

The address embossed on the letterhead is 15 Fitzjohn's Avenue, N.W. 3. Bernard lived there as an only child with his parents in one of those large Victorian redbrick houses that are now divided into flats and studios. Win lived nearby on Parsifal Road, in a similar house, only smaller. Both of their fathers were stockbrokers in the City of London. Richard Schlesinger was the more successful; known among his colleagues as Richard the Thirteenth, he was reputedly able to squeeze thirteen pence out of a shilling, which, as some people might recall, was worth only twelve. Win's father, Herman Regensburg, was said to have been more interested in music than in stocks.

Music was the centre of family life among many Hampstead Jews. Music was a sign of education, high culture an emblem of class. This was the way it had been in Germany, where a classical education was the indispensable mark of the high bourgeoisie, the *Bildungsbürger*. Hampstead is where the Jewish *Bildungsbürger* lived. Fitzjohn's Avenue was also known, perhaps not always kindly, as "Fitzjews Avenue."

Music is the common subject of the first letters. It is also how my grandparents met. Win was giving a violin recital on a Sunday afternoon at the home of Leo Fernberg, Bernard's cousin, who was also in love with her, an unhappy situation that would cause some tension between the two men. Various uncles and aunts and cousins—the Sterns, the Ellingers, the Seligmans, the Schwabs—would have been there, having tea and cakes. English was no doubt the common language, even though a smattering of German—never, never Yiddish—might have been spoken too. I once met one of the Ellinger aunts at a very advanced age; she remembered Richard Schlesinger as being "very British" and wearing a green suit.

His letter continues:

The finest concert of the week was yesterday's, Saturday's, and by far the most beautiful work I have heard for a long time & one of the most beautiful I have ever heard was Brahms's Requiem. The [Beethoven's] IXth . . . was grand & thrilling all the way through. The last movement sweeps all before it and carries you right through God Save the King, out of Queen's Hall onto No. 13 bus where you are only awakened to your senses by being barged into by a Tommie on your left & squashing a lady on your right & you realize at last that the world is not all "Freude schöner Götterfunken."

Indeed, the world was not all "Joy, lovely divine light." The war had been going on for almost a year already. The poster of Lord Kitchener pointing his finger, with the words "Your country needs you" in blood-red letters, was everywhere. Many thousands of young men all over Europe were joining up for the grandest war of all time in a spirit of great patriotic excitement. But for an Anglo-German family things must have been a little complicated. Even though some letters from relatives in Germany still miraculously got through, Bernard's father in particular was depressed about the war between his adopted and native countries.

Win too was often melancholy. Her bouts of gloominess, shared by her father and some of her future offspring, were known in the family, with a typical reference to Wagner's *Ring*, as "the curse of the Regensburgs." The tone of her letters is still rather formal at this stage:

May 14:

Dear Bernard,

I must just write a few words to thank you for your
post-card; it was awfully jolly of you to think of me . . .
everything is so frantically depressing at home, that it is
almost impossible to breathe. I have actually not got the
heart to practice. I have scarcely looked at my fiddle,
except when I have to play at college. Now I really must
shut myself up, or I shall be depressing you as well. I
promised to write about concerts, & I have written
nothing but complaints.

It was Bernard's customary role to cheer her up. She would
always recall that she fell in love with him on first sight, because of the broad grin on his face when he entered the drawing room carrying a cello on that Sunday afternoon at the
Fernbergs'. If she was prone to dwell on the shadows of life, he
could be relied upon to see the sunny side, even at times when
there was little brightness to be seen.

Bernard's letter of May 26 is sent from his school, Uppingham, not one of the poshest public schools, but a respectable
establishment with a solid reputation. Bernard, gregarious and
keen on games, adored his schooldays. He played rugby for the
first XV, a sure sign of schoolboy success, and was head of his
house, something that both (especially Win) would recall with
pride. Boris Karloff, the Hollywood monster, and Ronald Fir-
bank, master of the camp novel (*Prancing Nigger* et al.), had

Bernard at Uppingham

been at Uppingham a few years before Bernard, but I rather doubt that they took their status as Old Uppinghamians as seriously as he did.

Bernard tries to make Win laugh with a story of being reprimanded for grinning in chapel, but then tells her something that she would find quite unsettling:

> I am awfully bucked in a way. It is now definitely
> settled that I am leaving at the end of this term.

He adds, "In orchestra we are doing all English music. It's quite pretty, some of it. [The music master] calls it 'healthy.'

Why this epithet I can't imagine. I wonder if he considers Beethoven—night-marey & Brahms—indigestible?"

The music master may have been a little extreme. But the mood in Britain was more hysterically anti-German in 1915 than in 1940. Germans—the Bosch,* the Huns—were the enemies in the Great War. Nazis were the focus of hatred in the later war, and the music master's attitude would probably have struck more people as excessive.

Win's reply, of May 28, from 17 Parsifal Road:

Dear Bernard,

Thank you very much for your ripping letter; it had the desired effect, & cheered me up considerably. There is only one thing about which I cannot agree with you; I fail to be bucked that you are leaving school this term. Does that mean that you are going to join the RAMC [Royal Army Medical Corps] at once, or will you stop at home for a bit? In any case, I hope you will need plenty of training before you will go to the front.

I don't know when Bernard had decided to become a doctor, but he certainly never showed any interest in stockbroking. Joining the RAMC must have been his own idea. Perhaps he was especially keen to demonstrate his patriotism, in light of his family background. In any case, he signed up before the

---

*This derogatory word for the Germans can be spelled in different ways: "Bosch," "Bosche," or "Boche." The last is the most common. Bernard always used "Bosch."

end of term. In June, while still at school, he was taking first aid lessons with masters' wives and other local women. But even though his loyalty to England was never in doubt, even at his very young age he was irritated by the extreme hostility towards everything German, far more irritated, not surprisingly, than he would be by anti-German sentiments in World War II:

> My 'Cello master, an awful sport, who has been at
> Uppingham 17 years & far longer than the beastly old
> Headmaster is going to be given the sack because he is a
> naturalized German. Typical of the narrow Head-man!

Aside from his first aid classes, Bernard was preparing for his entrance exams to Cambridge. But he worries that he will never get there because of the war: "Don't you think it's a dirty trick?"

She replies, in her neat young girlish handwriting, that she is "very, very sorry to see from your letter, that you are troubled by the thought that you might never get to Cambridge at all. You mustn't get down in the dumps, or even let such thoughts enter your head. Personally, I am hoping for all I am worth, that some miracle will intervene to stop this beastly war, before any of you boys have to go."

On July 15, Bernard thinks he is finally off to the battle-front, a piece of news that he conveys in his usual facetious schoolboy style. The letter is sent from Uppingham:

> Mille remerciments pour votre lettre dernière. This
> is what will have to be in a few weeks. Goodbye to old

Bernard (SECOND FROM LEFT) *on a visit to Uppingham*
before being sent to France

English & start life afresh with broken—perhaps beyond
repair—French. I ought to be out there in three weeks or
so as an orderly under a doctor who has gone out from
here to be head surgeon at a hospital in Havre. Under
us—a friend is probably going out with me—are to be six
unruly French orderlies described as the "limit" & all
around us to all accounts are to be rats and smells.
Thrilling, n'est ce pas?

One month later, Private Schlesinger, RAMC, is still in England, billeted with a police constable and his wife in Great
Missenden, Buckinghamshire, "sitting, never before so careless

and irresponsible, smoking my wee pipe, whilst imagining all
the smells and the rats that might have been."

The training, he assures her, "promises to be very interesting & not too strenuous." On one of the "stretcher-drills," he
has to pretend to be a wounded soldier lying in a wood: "I was
jolly glad I wasn't really wounded, otherwise I am sure that by
the time they had decided what to do with me, they would no
longer have needed a stretcher but rather a couple of spades to
dig my grave. And so my life continues until further notice, and
a jolly one it will be I'm sure."

The jocular tone, though characteristic, might have dis-
guised a degree of nervous apprehension. But Bernard didn't
yet have a clear idea of what the actual battlefront was like. In
fact, he was impatient to be sent to France as soon as possible.
The drills reminded him of military training he had done for
years at school. On August 24, a letter is sent from the RAMC
headquarters at Great Missenden. He complains that his cap
doesn't fit his large head, even though recruiting posters everywhere bear the message "If the cap fits, join to-day."

It was one of these posters that attracted him to his later
regiment, the Queen's Westminster Rifles. A strapping young
soldier in khaki puttees smiles from the picture as if inviting
one and all to a grand party. Bernard liked the look of him. He
actually met the man in the picture by pure chance during the
war and they became lifelong friends. His name was Harry, a
silversmith in civilian life. In the letter of August 24, there is a
mention of another friend, from school, named Sharp, whom
Bernard is trying to get to share his billet. The effort elicits a
peculiar remark:

Still so far I am unable to get my friend down & stand
in danger of having a fellow named Cohen—who is very
Coheny—as my co-billeter.

To interpret this as anti-Semitism (or self-hatred, if you prefer) would be misleading. In fact, it is more likely a matter
of class. Bernard was not a snob. He refused to become an officer, preferring a place in the ranks. But Cohen was most
likely not from Fitzjohn's Avenue, or Parsifal Road, but from
Whitechapel perhaps, or the Leylands in Leeds, areas where
poorer, more religious Jews lived. In any case, Cohen was too
obviously Jewish for Bernard's taste. Perhaps he even had a
foreign-sounding accent.

Bernard's own foreign name caused enough difficulties,
but he makes light of this:

> I've never in my life had such a variety of names as
> here—not even at Uppingham. The Sgt. Major knocks off
> at 6:30 during Physical Drill with the tennis ball maker's
> name [Slazenger]. I come home to breakfast and get
> "Good morning, Mr." . . . . . . & that's as far as Mr. and
> Mrs. P[olice] C[onstable] get with it. During the course
> of the next parade I am called the following varying
> concoctions & contusions by the men—Bernard (with the
> emphasis on the second syllable), Schles, Slesi, Schlosh,
> Schlosly & many others.

Nothing much happens in the summer of 1915. He is bored
in Great Missenden. She goes off for a family holiday to a

rented house in the country. And always the exchanges return to music: "Cook has gone up to London," Win relates, so she and her elder brother, my great-uncle Walter, and her sister, Meg, have to fend for themselves, having drinks "to the accompaniment of a Haydn trio. We made the beds to a Brahms quintet, & cooked dinner with doses of Schubert & Beethoven trios. I am sure no cook-house-parlour maids ever worked to such classical stuff before."

There are photographs of this trip, not much bigger than postage stamps, showing Win, petite in the midst of her siblings and aunts, a walking stick in her right hand, dressed in a tweed skirt and sporting a beret at a jaunty angle. They all seem in fine spirits, laughing at the camera. There is not a hint of war. The jollity on the surface is what makes these pictures, and much else about the first years of the war, so chilling.

On September 6, Bernard writes a letter from Oxford, where he has his first glimpse of the real consequences of the war. He attended an organ recital in Christ Church Cathedral, "the first programme of decent music I've heard since I played for the last time in the Uppingham Gym. at the end of my last term, years ago it seems to me now. It <u>was</u> a treat & such a change from comic songs and marching twaddle."

But then:

We were up till twelve the night before watching a convoy of wounded arrive & bearing them from their bunks in the train on stretchers to the ambulance motors. It is quite a thrilling sight to see and help a convoy arrive. The platform is cleared of everybody but RAMC & St.

John's ambulance men. On the platform are piled up stretchers, pillows, blankets & trolleys. Doctors are in preparation & groups of RAMC men are talking impatiently in groups & are preparing the stretchers. Outside the station are lined up ambulances, and kind ladies with milk & very watery lemonade (I tasted it).

A train steams thro' the station & at the windows are massed all those who can stand swathed in various bandages & slings. They cheer and seem very jolly. You hardly think they are the wounded until the train backs into a siding and slowly comes to a halt. We go to the bad cases first & stretcher after stretcher is taken into the specially fitted up compartments in the front of the train and comes out loaded with some poor beggar who doesn't care at all for his wounds but is only glad to be back in England . . .

We have been down here a week now & are staying about another. I am sublimely happy amongst the sick & have picked up quite a lot about dressings etc.

They are all awfully cheery and brave and the same advice comes from all: "You stay this side of the water, mate, as long as you b—— well can."

In the evenings one of the nurses plays ragtimes by ear and we sing lustily. In this manner they & you speedily forget their suffering.

There is plenty of it & and you just begin to realize the absolute wickedness, barbarity &—— there is nothing bad enough to term it—of the war, when you see these terrible wounds & hear the moaning when they are dressed.

Winnie responds the next day. You might have expected her to be even more worried after his description of the wounded. Instead, her tone is full of youthful idealism. His letter has made her "long desperately to be able to do something to help, like you are doing. It must be a glorious feeling every night when you go to bed, however tired you are, to think that you have spent your whole day in trying to make other people's suffering less, & I think, more and more, how much finer your work is than all the commissions in the world."

Winnie wanted to become a nurse and do her bit for the war effort. After finishing her schooling at South Hampstead High School for girls, she was taking cookery lessons as well as studying the violin on a music scholarship. She decides to resign the scholarship for the time being and take a course in first aid and other nursing skills. The lectures on these topics, given by Dr. Cantlie, "a dear old Scottie" who had once taught Sun Yat-sen in Hong Kong, she finds "fearfully amusing."

It was at about this time that my great-uncle Walter, Winnie's elder brother, decided to change his family name from Regensburg to Raeburn, suggesting a Scottish provenance. The motive was not to get rid of a Jewish name, but of a German one.

Bernard worried that "the name" was delaying his chances of being sent to the front. One day, the sergeant major at Great Missenden read out sixteen names of men who would be shipped to France imminently. Bernard's name wasn't among them. But, ever the optimist, he still felt confident that "my turn will come some time." He wondered, however, in a letter dated September 30, 1915, "if the name of Regensburg will hinder you at all in getting work at a hospital. I think 'Schlesinger' did some of the harm in my case . . . Perhaps you will be Raeburn in hospital."

In fact, she never did become a Raeburn. Nor would she follow her elder brother in his conversion to the Church of England after the war. Walter, a keen public schoolboy (Charterhouse), like Bernard, was also waiting to be sent to where the action was. He did not have to wait quite as long. Sent to the front line at Ypres, he was badly wounded in 1916.

It appears that Winnie's age might have been more of a professional impediment than her name; only eighteen, she was by far the youngest person to attend Dr. Cantlie's lectures in first aid. She couldn't wait to get into the sky-blue and white uniform of a Voluntary Aid Detachment (VAD) nurse. But since there was an oversupply of volunteers, she thought that she stood little chance. A friend of her mother's, named Mrs. Kaminski, sought the advice of the matron of a Hampstead hospital. The matron promised to take Winnie into her ward "in spite of my name," as soon as she got her nursing certificate, but this quickly fell through. So perhaps it was "the name" after all.

On November 6, she writes about another opportunity opening up, at a place called Beech House Military Hospital in Brondesbury:

> The door was opened to me by a V.A.D. whose features told me distinctly that her name must end in

"burg" or "stein." I saw several of the same description,
so I thought things looked promising.

The German origin of her parents didn't worry the authorities at Beech House unduly. The hospital was in fact entirely
staffed by Jews. I found a reference to it in a history of World
War I hospitals in London. Beech House was closed in 1919.
The building still stands, as a private residence. True to the
north-west London Jewish milieu that permeated the place, the
hospital was proudly British. Patients "were encouraged to garden and would also hold cricket matches against the nearby
Brondesbury Park Military Hospital."

About the national loyalties of Winnie and Bernard there
was never any ambivalence. But I have often wondered what it
must have been like for their parents. Neither Winnie's father
nor Bernard's left Germany because of persecution, even
though the financial crash in 1873 had been blamed on "Jewish
speculators," which meant that all Jews were potential targets
of popular wrath. I read somewhere in an account of our family
history that in public places my German ancestors would always refer to Jews as "Italians," to avoid drawing unwelcome
attention to themselves. Still, the main reason they had left
Germany was that there were better job opportunities in the
City of London. I know that Herman Regensburg still liked to
spend his summer holidays in the Black Forest, and Richard
Schlesinger liked nothing better than to tell German jokes over
a rubber of skat, a German card game invented in the nineteenth century (Richard Strauss was said to have been a keen
skat player). Some of these jokes are quoted in Bernard's letters.

Win (ON THE RIGHT) with her brother, Walter,
and sister, Margaret

Even though he always professed, in English gentlemanly fashion, not to speak foreign languages, except for some horribly
mangled French, the jokes are in perfect vernacular German.
They were not repeated after World War I.

I have a photograph of Richard Schlesinger, my great-
grandfather, taken in the early 1880s, looking proud and dash-
ing in his Prussian army uniform, sporting a Kaiser Wilhelm
moustache. (It is true, however, that Jews, despite having equal
rights in theory, almost never became officers before World
War I. According to Schlesinger family lore, quite possibly
apocryphal, Richard decided to emigrate after a friend replied
to his innocent question as to why he wasn't being promoted,
"But, Richard, you are a Jew.")

There is a reference to Richard's mood in a letter dated
October 19, 1915. A pianist named Wulston Holmes was enter-

taining the Schlesinger family on a Sunday afternoon at Fitz-john's Avenue. Known for his skill as an improviser, Holmes was also a composer of moody pieces with such titles as "Disappointment" or "A Dream." He had been playing for two solid hours when Bernard asked him, a little morbidly given the circumstances, whether he had ever composed a funeral march. Holmes replied that he had not as yet, and "played one there and then on the spur of the moment." Bernard thought it was "absolutely divine and not even in this could he be sad. It was an uplifting funeral march which would really make you die a cheerful death."

Not so surprisingly, however, "father looked rather glum and so I asked [Holmes] if for father's benefit he would play an anti-war tonic. A romping, cheery piece was immediately forthcoming & even father forgot the war for a few minutes."

Of course, Richard Schlesinger's gloominess may have had more to do with the fear of losing his only child than with any residual nostalgia for his native country. And there are more hints in Bernard's letters that he too had at least some inkling of what might be waiting for him.

On November 4 he mentions "a wet morning," when he spoke to a corporal with malaria "from our first unit back from the Dardanelles [in other words, Gallipoli, where more than forty thousand Allied soldiers were killed and many more wounded]." The soldier "talked of his experiences for three hours. By Jove, it made us realize what we were booked for,—not a picnic."

But the thought of horror is immediately dispelled by his casual schoolboy jauntiness: "Talking of picnics after this

Bernard with his friend Sharp

world's mess-up is over, and we RAMC have finished cleaning it up, we must try and repeat our picnic." And he recalls a happy memory of a joint lunch on Hampstead Heath.

The first photograph of Bernard in uniform is enclosed in a letter sent on November 11, evidently at Win's request. It shows him with his friend Sharp. Already quite shortsighted, Bernard squints through a pair of rimless glasses. His large mouth is pulled into a lopsided grin. The simple private's uniform appears to fit a little too tightly around his squat rugby player's body. At the bottom of the photograph is a rather cryptic sentence written in his scrawl: "Just two minds with but one single thought." It is not immediately clear whether this refers to Win or to Sharp.

On balance, I think, it must be Win whose mind shares a single thought, as she thanks him for the photo in her next letter and asks him to write something on it. If so, it is the first declaration of a special intimacy in between reports on first aid courses, army drills, rugger matches, and music:

Dear Bernard,
    I am going to write to you now, while I am still
inspired with glorious music. We have been playing
Beethoven and Mozart string quintets all the afternoon,
& of course I was in seventh heaven.

A photograph of Win is enclosed, taken by Estella Heymans in her Hampstead studio. She looks a trifle solemn, perhaps a little older than her years, but beautiful, in a pre-Raphaelite way, with her thick dark hair, a generous mouth, and large baby-blue eyes. It was the best of the bunch, she writes, but her family hated the picture. Perhaps Bernard should just return it. Then follows an exchange that clearly shows that they are now in love. The tone would be repeated in many variations in letters for the rest of their lives.

December 6, Winnie to Bernard:

    I missed a letter from you. I had been so looking
forward to one, & am disappointed that it never came . . .
I have got crowds to tell you about all my experiences,
but I shall wait until I know whether you want to
hear it.

December 7, Bernard to Win:

Winnie, how can you imagine for an instant that I
don't want to hear how you fared . . . Of course I wrote
you a long epistle . . . I wonder whatever can have
happened to it? I hope it is not lost.

December 7, Win to Bernard:

It has come! It arrived this morning . . . Please forget
everything that I wrote yesterday. I was feeling so miserable
& down in the dumps, & I am afraid I was beastly to
everyone I saw. I couldn't imagine why I hadn't heard a
word from you since I saw you last.

December 13, Win to Bernard:

I don't know if you realize that you have not been to
our house properly (to a meal) since Northwood. Do your
people object to your coming here, or why is it?

December 17, Bernard to Win:

Before we proceed, I want to set your mind at rest
over one point. Of course my people don't object to my
coming to The Mountain of Roses [Rosemount was the

name of Win's house on Parsifal Road], but they don't
love my going anywhere but home for any length of time.

Bernard then breaks into a string of lyrical clichés that
always marked moments of high emotion, of elation or despair;
it was as if his love of Wagner, and especially James Barrie,
author of *Peter Pan*, was reflected in a gushing stream of
sentiment, which was nonetheless too deeply felt to be called
sentimental:

> And now, oh glorious day, we are having Xmas
> leave . . . So we can have an afternoon together after all
> before the end of the war. A proper time, mark you. I
> wish somehow the "tons" [of things she had to tell him]
> could be aired under a dark starry Heaven with all the
> trees & houses silhouetted in a dim background where
> even the ugliest object is made beautiful in its vesture of
> shadows & the moon shines down complacent with its
> peaceful light & turns down for the benefit of mankind a
> smiling white face pleased only at its own handiwork. Or
> failing this, a darkened room with just a fire . . . with a
> jolly flickering flame dancing . . . Just like your thoughts
> and dreams as you sit gazing idly into it. Either of these
> atmospheres are our mutual delight. Can't it be?

Then, a sudden switch of mood:

> Sharp has returned, the washing's finished & the spell
> has been broken.

Win in 1915

December 18, Win to Bernard:

Of course I know how hard it must be for your people
to let you go for one minute out of the short time you can
be with them, & I do really feel a pig every time I ask you
to come here. But then you see, sometimes I want you to
come so much that I let my feelings get the better of my
reason . . . Isn't it funny, although we have never spoken
about it, we both know so exactly what we mutually love.

Barely a week after this letter, even more abruptly than it
had begun, it all seemed suddenly to be over. I am not sure why

Bernard's parents decided that the budding liaison had to end. Because they were too young, probably. Because he was a cherished only child, perhaps. Religion cannot have been the reason, even though his father was an Orthodox Jew and his mother kept a kosher home, while the Regensburgs never went to synagogue at all. It certainly wasn't a matter of class. The Regensburgs sold musical instruments on the edge of the Altstadt (Old Town) of Frankfurt. Richard Schlesinger's father ran a textile business in the same city. The two fathers had actually been classmates in the same Gymnasium.

On Christmas Day, the letter arrived from Bernard. It is both cliché-ridden in the most cloying James Barrie manner, and heartbreaking. "Dear sweet Winnie," it begins. "This is going to be the hardest letter I ever had to write to anyone . . . I am going to hurt you very much. I have suffered this pain for a day and parts of two nights too, because I knew what I would have to do and I was worrying how I could do it in the least hurtful way to both of us."

Then come the painful metaphors and images plucked from Victorian childhood books of fairy tales and animal stories. He had been supremely happy the last time he saw her, when all of a sudden "in the blue sky of happiness a little black cloud appeared from nowhere & grew & grew & soon it overshadowed nearly all the blue."

He took the whole picture of the blue and the black to his parents—"the most wonderful people you have in the world, even more wonderful in their way than you, Winnie—& they made that black cloud clear."

They had made Bernard see that Win and he had been like

two "little field mice," one white and one bigger and brown. They talked and they talked, these mice who were much too young to know what they were getting into. It had all happened too fast, too soon.

They were like two blind moles, "blind in their love and happiness just as we might have been. Mr. Mole has also spoken too soon." He would "go down into a great hole into the world of toil and people." Miss Mole would stay behind and wait for his messages. He might find another Miss Mole, after he had grown older and wiser, and she would still be waiting. Should he return to her out of pity? Would it not have been better if he had broken away before it was too late?

They were like two "red squirrels in love," like the mice and the moles. But the big red squirrel could not continue to frolic in the trees and bathe in the sun and gather nuts and be a successful squirrel. This would not do: "Love, free but fettered serious love is not for a squirrel with only 19 years to his name. He will droop, he will not find his nuts & in the end will lose everything, & so will she."

And so Bernard's parents were surely right. Win would have to understand his mother's worries. They were not angry with her. His father had even observed that "any woman since Mrs. Eve, *selig*, would have done the same!"

All this would be funny, and possibly in retrospect it was, if it weren't so desperately sad. Here is how the letter ends:

> We all agreed that I had fallen in love with the
> right girl first. And so we are all just very good friends.
> Friends—boy and girl friends—may see each other

sometimes—not too often & not alone too often in our case—but they must not write.

If you want to do me the greatest turn you ever can & set our worrying to the nil, please, I beg you, do as I am going to do. Cheer up, enjoy the glorious world & see as many beings as you can. The future holds all else in its own grasp.

I am going to regard our little soul-speaking affair as the greatest & most gorgeous, delightfully happy dream I have ever had. Will you do the same, I implore you. Dreams come and faint away in mist, some are forgotten, some are remembered—the latter are the happy ones. Ours has been just like the IVth variation of the Beethoven Quartet I was thinking about last night. And, Winnie, some dreams come true.

I would very much like a word to know if you understand. Remember the greatest turn.

This will be the last "proper" word you will hear from me, perhaps forever. The chain has broken; haven't the "tons" come down with a crash?

Did it hurt very much?

Farewell little white field mouse.

Cheer up as I am going to do & once again & finally maybe forever,

Love from Bernard

Her answer, written the very next day, has none of his flowery metaphors. She expresses her raw emotion more plainly, more briskly, and it is all the more moving for that. The exchange upsets all stereotypes of male and female expression we might associate with people still born in the Victorian age:

> Oh Bernard, of course I understand, & I know it is all quite right. When I poured out all my happiness to Mother and Father after you had gone, Mother told me your squirrel story, word for word, & Father called it our "Probepfeil" [testing arrow]. But I didn't want to let them spoil our beautiful dream, & I dreamed on for another whole day. Now it is over. Bernard, I don't think you can realise one-millionth part of how it hurts, because you are only a dear, lovable, impulsive boy, and I am not a very impulsive woman.

This is where the correspondence ends. There are no more letters for many months. How it must have felt to be in limbo, having broken off relations with the girl he loved and waiting to be sent to the battlefront, is impossible to know, but easy to imagine. The silence is broken for the first time on June 18, 1916, in a letter formally addressed to Win's mother, Mrs. Regensburg, sent by Rifleman Schlesinger no. 6901, 2/16 Queen's Westminster Rifles, from Sandhill Camp, near Warminster, in Wiltshire. It is written in pencil.

Mrs. Regensburg is kindly thanked for sending him a compact medicine chest, and Bernard assures her that with this precious gift he can "do all sorts of things without harm." Gun shells may burst quite close to him, but "their subsequent effects—a headache or shaky nerves—will soon be counteracted by aspirin and nerve tonic."

He tells her how the men are all being made to crop their hair. Some, he reports, get the regimental barber to cut the regimental number on their heads with a fine pair of scissors. Others have an arrow carved out "to remind them they belong to the army."

Well, he concludes:

> I have dozens of people to whom I ought to write, so I had better wind up. Au revoir & love to all. Many thanks again.
>
>   Cheery oh, Bernard

The next letter to "Mrs. Regensburg," at Rosemount, 17 Parsifal Road, London, would arrive from the front lines of the battle on the Somme.

Two

GOING TO WAR

—·—

ernard never liked to talk about his experiences in World War I. Ever one to look at the bright side of things, he did not care to even mention the worst he had seen: no stories about men chased into German machine-gun fire by officers blowing whistles, like football referees; no stories of soldiers torn apart by mines, or screaming as they died slowly in the filthy muck of no man's land; of fresh corpses being eaten by bloated rats; of maggot-infested wounds and faces blown away; and so on, and on, into the unmentionable, or at least unimaginable, horrors of the war of attrition.

He did, come to think of it, often proclaim, perhaps a little facetiously, the excellence of bully beef stew, or plain "Bully," the most common and probably quite disgusting British army ration of tinned corned beef. Actually, even this luxury was rarely available on the front lines, where a soldier would be

Rifleman Schlesinger

lucky to get a slice of stale bread with margarine. And I never heard him use words like "fuck," since, as he once explained, he had heard so much swearing in the trenches that he had enough to last a lifetime. But that, apart from a few place names and a memory of marching into Jerusalem with General Allenby's troops, was about it.

It was a lot easier to talk about the second war, much of which Bernard spent charging around northern India as an army doctor. But about his time on the Somme he remained mute. Perhaps memories of World War II had crowded out those of the first war. Or possibly he had repressed them.

And yet repression, if that is what it was, was not complete. When I was still a very young boy, he was keen to pass on some of his relics of the Great War. I still have his RAMC cap badge, and his First Field Dressing, a small dun-coloured package, manufactured in Doncaster, containing a piece of gauze, a pad, and a bit of waterproof material. This was kept by every British and Empire soldier on the inside flap of his tunic. Quite how much it would help after a person was ripped apart by machine-gun fire or shrapnel, I don't know. An instruction on the package reads, "If two wounds, put the pad on one and the piece of gauze on the other and divide the waterproof."

I do remember Bernard mentioning that he was stationed somewhere around Arras, which would have put him near the infamous Vimy Ridge, the capture of which cost the British about 160,000 casualties. But that battle was in 1917, when he was fighting the Bulgarians in Greece.

I am not sure either what he was doing on July 1, that sickening first day of the Battle of the Somme when more than 20,000 British troops were killed and 40,000 wounded in a matter of hours, cut down by German machine guns after rushing over the tops of their trenches in wave after wave, fortified on empty stomachs by a tot of navy rum—you didn't want to be hit in the gut just after breakfast. French and British generals knew perfectly well that not much could be done in the summer of 1916 to break the stalemate on the Western Front. The only plan they had was to kill more Germans than the Germans could kill British and French. Four months later, the Allies had advanced about seven miles. By then, more than a

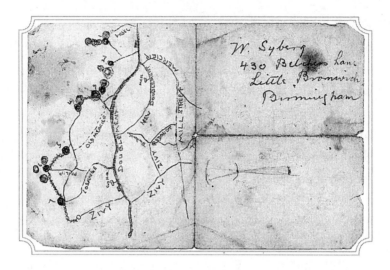

Map of Bernard's trench near the Somme

million German, French, and British Empire soldiers were
wounded or dead.

Amid Bernard's letters is a small map, drawn in blue and
red, of the trenches where the Second Battalion of the Queen's
Westminster Rifles huddled together with soldiers from the
Black Watch. I cannot imagine that anyone was allowed to
carry such sensitive information, but Bernard always had a terrible sense of direction, so perhaps he secretly bore this map so
he wouldn't wander off into no man's land. Or it could have
been drawn up later.

Several place names are scribbled on the map: Doublement,
Zivy, Mill Street, Mercier. The trench was indeed near Vimy
Ridge, in a place called Neuville-Saint-Vaast, four miles north
of Arras. By the time Bernard got there, the town was already a

pile of rubble. Henri Gaudier-Brzeska, the French sculptor, had been killed there the year before.

The QWR battalion's commanding officer, Lieutenant Colonel Gordon Clark, noted in his war diary that his troops, including Bernard, had landed in Le Havre from Southampton on June 23. On the thirtieth, they were in the trenches. On July 1 the diary notes, "Trenches. A + B company platoon in front line for instruction. Attached to 1/6 Black Watch."

There is a mention also of Vimy Ridge in a letter to Win written two years after the war, when Bernard talks about the warm companionship felt by human beings when huddling by a fire. "I suppose," he writes, "it's a throwback to our very ancient ancestors, yours and mine, who lived more or less wild in the open." Then he remembers the "little Stretcher Bearer dugout in the front line near Vimy where Harry, a fellow called Finlow, and I used to sit on our haunches hunched up but comfortable and secure. A candle stuck into the muddy wall was our fire then and we discoursed into its flickering flame and stopped to relight it occasionally as the rush of air from some passing Bosch shell thumped it out."

This sounds rather more casual than it would have been on most nights. The British journalist Robert Kee once described the trenches as "the concentration camps of World War One." John Keegan, in whose marvellous book *The Face of Battle* these words are quoted, remarks that this analogy is not quite exact historically, but that "there is something Treblinka-like about almost all accounts of July 1st, about those long docile lines of young men, shoddily uniformed, heavily burdened, numbered about their necks, plodding forward across a featureless landscape to their own extermination inside the barbed wire."

Bernard was still in the trenches on July 7, the date of his first letter. He speaks of the roasting-hot weather, interrupted by rainstorms that flooded the trenches and turned the terrain into liquid mud. His letter, written in pencil to "Rosemount," the house on 17 Parsifal Road, is addressed to "All of you" (direct correspondence between Bernard and Win is still scrupulously avoided). The striking thing about the letter is how much is left unsaid. A stiff-upper-lipped, even perky tone is maintained throughout.

He writes, "We have had our first spell in the trenches and of course our company were reported to have got in the way of things quickest and best." Quite what those "things" were isn't mentioned, but they could be imagined. The First Battalion of the Queen's Westminster Rifles formed part of an almost suicidal attack on the German trenches in Gommecourt. When survivors of the first waves ran out of ammunition, they had to find extra bullets on the corpses of their murdered comrades floating in waterlogged bomb craters or caught in barbed wire.

Bernard doesn't mention any of this, nor where he is, for military censors would have deleted such information at once. He writes as though he were reporting a rugger match at Uppingham, but a few details do seep through: "It is some life out here I can tell you & certainly an experience not to be missed, from a sweaty digging fatigue under a hot sun & stray whizz bangs [high-velocity German artillery] somewhere more or less near, to a muddy dugout with rats & communication trenches with water up to your knees in places."

It would take him twenty-seven years to spell out more con-
cretely what it actually meant to be a stretcher bearer on the
Western Front in 1916. On February 17, 1943, sitting in a military hospital in Delhi, feeling lonely and impatient for the war
to end, he writes a letter to his wife:

> On waking this morning I was trying to recall the
> most stirring events of my life and it hadn't to go very far
> before it became our life. Let's see what are some of
> them. Going back to schooldays—hearing my name
> announced at the end of a match & going through the
> rituals of receiving my first XV colours. My letter to you
> putting our "understanding" into cold storage is not such
> a pretty memory, but I can see myself now seated in the
> carpentry room composing it. Then came the war so full
> of stirring adventures that they have merged into a blur
> but one occasion has always stood out preeminently &
> that was having to dig out the human mess from a dugout
> that had received a direct hit.

There may have been more letters sent in July 1916, for the
next one in my possession, dated August 3, mentions that "life
here is much the same—you must know the life well by now."
Or perhaps he is just referring to fragments of knowledge in
England about the battlefronts with all the horrors glossed over.
Apart from telling jokes and thanking the inhabitants of Parsifal Road for a delicious chocolate cake and a tin of cream, which
were mailed to the front (how they survived in the field post
God only knows), he gives a hint of his life as a stretcher bearer:

Carrying long stretchers down narrow trenches not made for them is slightly different from the performance at Great Missenden or on Salisbury Plain. Were our old staff Sgt. to see the necessary rough rides patients have to undergo, he'd go grey I believe.

After Bernard's death, a Mr. Stewart Nicoll recalled in a letter of condolence that Bernard had "saved many lives; probably mine too, for he was one of the two stretcher bearers who got me out of the labyrinth. Shortly afterwards he became the medical orderly; many I know thought him better than the doctor."

From the way he played squash or tennis with me, when he was well into his seventies, I can picture his young face as he strained to rush wounded men through the trenches, his lips tight with concentration, a heavy sweat on his reddened brow. But in his letters he manages to turn even the most severe discomfort into a kind of joke. On September 3, a month of many raids on enemy trenches, often resulting in hand-to-hand combat with bayonets, he recalls how "we nearly got drowned in our dugout the other day & I swear I saw a periscope but we rammed it with a shovel & the U-boat sank to the bottomless depths. I hear tapioca mentioned down below. I wonder if it's sticky. Well, cheery oh for now."

Cakes, sticky puddings, U-boat jokes. This is true to his chirpy outlook, but I don't think his tone was particularly unusual, especially for a young Englishman of his class and education. Such men were supposed to make light of their hardships; it was part of the British ethos. Much has been writ-

ten about the so-called public school officers and their attitudes to king, country, and the war itself, which was treated by
some of them, at least in the initial stages, as a kind of game.
There are stories of public school heroes kicking a football as
they made their fatal dash into German machine-gun fire.

Bernard was not an officer in World War I. He chose to
remain a private. But the attitude—the stoicism, the good
humour, the unquestioned patriotism, the unshakeable sense of
duty—was something he clearly wished to live up to. This type
of fortitude was at once admirable and frighteningly naïve. For
it left a generation of men vulnerable to propaganda that would
lead them more or less eagerly to the slaughter. There were of
course men of Bernard's class, often of a literary or political
bent, who saw through the official pronouncements about the
British "spirit." But Bernard was not inclined to question it.
Embodying the right spirit was the core of his identity. It was
how he chose to see himself, and how he wished to be seen by
others.

At the beginning of November 1916, Bernard's company
had left the trenches. Billets were found in barns and farm-
houses, where the soldiers were taken care of by Madame This
or That, French ladies who did everything from cooking their
meals to darning their socks. He describes an afternoon at the
nearest town (Arras, perhaps), where the QWR rankers entered
a tea shop full of officers, "and so for an evening we feasted our
eyes on soldiers of all nations, bowler hats, lights, shops & some
sort of traffic other than limbers, country carts & staff cars."

The rest of this letter consists of a few almost unintelligible
army jokes, and more profuse thanks for packages of fruit,

cream, and cakes that found their way to the front. "There is not much else to tell you," he concludes, "except that before the end of this war we may see a bit more of ——." The last word is erased by a smudge of ink, either by Bernard or, more likely, by the military censor. Quite what place name or event the people at Rosemount were not allowed to see will forever be a mystery.

In November 1916, Bernard's company was transferred to "Muckydonia," as the soldiers liked to call the mosquito-infested ravines of Macedonia where British, French, Greek, and Serbian troops were fighting the Bulgarian allies of Germany and the Ottoman Empire. They had boarded ship in Marseilles on November 18, stopped at Malta on the twenty-third for several days ("officers only allowed on shore"), and arrived at Salonika on the thirtieth. The QWRs were now part of the British Salonika Force.

The Macedonia front has been described as 99 percent boredom and 1 percent hell. One of the problems was the weather, described quite vividly by Bernard in his first letter, dated December 8, 1916: "The weather out here certainly goes in for extremes. The night before last it came down in such torrents that our tents in the morning were separated from the field kitchens by a huge stream which had sprung up from nowhere. The mess orderlies consequently had to paddle across for our breakfast & one man, so I'm told, and several boxes of S[mall] A[rms] A[mmunition]—heavy things—floated away merrily." But, he continues, "the heavens soon get fed up with pouring forth and blowing out their cheeks & the next day it's as boiling hot as an English July."

Since he is still in Salonika, a city with a largely Jewish population that would be entirely wiped out by the Nazis less than
three decades later, and the long trek into the mountain region
is yet to begin, he doesn't mention the swarms of mosquitoes
that would soon infect and kill thousands of men with malaria.

Instead, he reminisces about his first driving lessons in
London given by his father's chauffeur, named Graham, who
instructed him in "the management of the Rolls." Graham too
was now enlisted in the army as a subaltern. Apparently he had
had little confidence in Bernard's driving skills, "especially
after a certain occasion when it was either us or a heavy horse
lorry who was to take preference at the Baker Street crossing. Rather hastily I chose the former & the lorry driver only
just managed to stop his horses from nibbling the top of mother's hat."

Ah, those old times. There is a hint, but only a hint, of what
was yet to come when he thanks "Rosemount" (still not Win)
for a pair of mitt-gloves, which "will come in very handy I
expect <u>when</u> we move up (—in every sense of the word—) the
line."

"Up" meant up into the hills, towards the sinister terrain
around Doiran Lake, where strongly fortified Bulgarian positions surveyed the valley from their flinty mountain redoubt,
known to the British as Pip Ridge, with an observation post
called the Devil's Eye. To get there, Allied soldiers often had to
build roads first. In the rocky ravines, the British then dug—or
literally blasted—filthy trenches as best they could, half sub-
merged in cages of barbed wire. The tactics were pretty much
the same as on the Western Front: a barrage of artillery fire

would supposedly smash the enemy positions, after which their trenches could be stormed by bayonet-wielding infantrymen.

What happened between April 22, when the Battle of Doiran began, and May 9, when it was abandoned, was more like the desperate Allied assault on the Dardanelles when more than forty thousand British, Australian, and New Zealand troops died while trying to claw their way up the Turkish-held cliffs of Gallipoli. The hundred thousand Allied shells, many of them filled with toxic gas, fired at the Bulgarians did little damage. The rocky mountain fortress was impregnable and the valley proved to be a death trap.

Mortars raining on the British in the narrow ravine caused such shock waves that soldiers were smashed against the rocks. Men who had made it, despite all the odds, to the mountain slopes, on top of which the Bulgarians were blasting away with machine guns and howitzers, were taunted with cries of "Come on, Johnny!" while being blown apart with bullets and hand grenades. In the valley, men were pinned down in trenches and bomb craters for days, most of them without access to food or drink, tormented by the mosquitoes, soaked by rainstorms or sweltering in the heat, and vomiting from the incoming gas shells. Anyone who raised his head was liable to get it blown off. And yet, as happened in France and the Dardanelles, each failure to overrun the enemy prompted another equally deadly and futile attempt, as if pure British pluck would ensure victory in the end. Until, in May, with more than ten thousand dead, the Allies finally gave up.

In a rare instance of old-fashioned chivalry, the Bulgarians once in a while allowed British stretcher bearers to run out in daylight to pick up the corpses strewn across the ravine after one more disastrous nocturnal attack. In his book *The Story of the Salonica Army*, G. Ward Price writes that "our doctors and stretcher-bearers with great gallantry stepped out directly into the open, trusting to no other protection than the Red Cross."

The stretcher bearers and medical orderlies had to cope for days and nights without much sleep with a continuous stream of wounded and mangled men, who still had a chance of survival in the dressing stations.

One of the orderlies was Bernard. There are no letters from the front at Doiran Lake. But his unit was certainly there. In the two letters from Macedonia that I have (there might possibly have been more), there is of course no mention of what he actually thought of this deadly clash between empires provoked by Balkan politics that few of the soldiers on either side would have even remotely understood. There is only one observation about the Greek allies, before the great battle began, showing that he was quite conventional in his prejudices: "Many have been our adventures, including a good insight into the lazy Greek & his ways & especially an interesting type of these people who has been to America some time or other & thus speaks broken English & uses the word 'sure' perfectly pronounced once in every five words."

By September 7, 1917, his battalion had been moved to Palestine via Egypt. There is a photograph of Bernard, looking rather unhappy, sitting cross-legged in shorts and a tropical helmet on the back of a camel in front of the pyramid of Giza. Because of the desert wind, Bernard finds the heat in Palestine quite bearable. To stave off the boredom of waiting for the next

Bernard (FAR RIGHT) in Egypt

military move, the men keep desert pets, anything from "colossal Tarantula spiders as big as a small rat to tiny little mice the size of a kitchen beetle." One officer keeps a chameleon, another a couple of field rats. One chap has a snake. He is nice, writes Bernard, but "that goes without saying—He's Irish & all Hibernians I have met are great."

Bernard does not mention what for, but an Old Uppinghamian "I knew slightly at school has just figured amongst the new list of V.C.s [Victoria Crosses]." He was "quite a nice, quiet, unassuming individual when I knew him. I suppose that's what 'The right stuff' is made from."

As would be the case so often in his life, Bernard's emotions are most deeply stirred by music. Here is his postscript to a letter written on September 10:

Last night we went to a Brigade concert & amongst
other items a Cello [player] appeared. Of course he
was out of practice, but not having heard a Cello since
Blighty—fifteen months ago!!! & the idea of an endless
vista of sand containing such an instrument gave it an
exceptional value.

When the cellist started playing Handel's Largo in G, Bernard was deeply touched, since it reminded him of the musical
afternoon when he first met Win, and he pictured himself
"struggling through the same piece vainly trying to remember
a few bars by heart, endeavouring with like futility to make it
sound nice & getting hot in the combined effort."

The next letter, dated December 6, is posted from Alexandria, where he had the luxury of writing in pen and ink instead
of the usual scrawl in pencil. He had been moved there from
the desert to have his tonsils removed: "Just tonsillitis, but they
shifted me from Beersheba to Alex, glad for the rest yet rather
ashamed & inclined to hang my tail between my legs at leaving
the rest of the boys in the middle of things."

"Things" in this instance meant the Battle of Beersheba.
Various attempts had been made by the British to capture Gaza
from the Turkish Ottoman troops, all of them ending in disaster with thousands of casualties. General Edmund Allenby
took over from the hapless Sir Archibald Murray. The problem
was that the Allied forces were stuck in the desert without access to water. Beersheba had wells. So the plan was to capture
Beersheba in a day, before the retreating Turkish defenders
had time to destroy the wells.

On October 31, the Turkish trenches were bombarded for several hours in the early morning, after which a combined force of British, Australian, and New Zealand troops attacked. By the afternoon more than a thousand Allied soldiers were dead, but the Turkish trenches were taken. Beersheba itself, however, was still in Ottoman hands.

When the sun began to set, the Australian general Harry Chauvel decided on a now legendary act of derring-do. Two Australian regiments of the Light Horse Brigade were ordered to storm Beersheba in an old-fashioned cavalry charge. Five hundred shouting and screaming Australians galloped through clouds of desert dust kicked up by the horses. Their bayonets, brandished like sabres, more for show than anything else, caught the last flickering rays of the sun. A number of horses and men crumpled under machine-gun fire, but the surprise was so great that the Turkish and German troops were overwhelmed, and after some ferocious hand-to-hand combat in the town, Beersheba was taken with its water wells intact.

Bernard refers to the battle obliquely. In a letter sent on December 6, Win's birthday, but still addressed to all in Parsifal Road, he mentions seeing a film in an Alexandria cinema about the fall of Beersheba (*La prise de Bir Saba*). He remarks, "I saw many things go up to the place of deployment on the night before [the attack] but never a Kinematograph. Still, one never knows it may have come up with the Bully [beef stew], but more likely the operator may have taken a few camels way back & there were plenty of them knocking about—ten thousand came up one night with supplies in one never ending column."

The letter ends with a special greeting: "As it's December 6th shall we all join in with the other blue-coated patients of Beech House in wishing the best of luck to the wee nurse of no. 6 ward & the rest of her family. Cheery oh everybody. Love, Bernard."

This is the first direct reference to Win in the wartime correspondence. Perhaps that is why it elicited a direct answer written on December 30, thanking Bernard:

> It was ripping of you to remember my birthday—I hope you are feeling quite fit again, but all the same, it was a pity you didn't manage more than three weeks in hospital. It was not long for tonsillitis, & anyhow you should have tried the useful and persuasive art of swinging the lead. I should think you'd be jolly well justified after—how many months is it?—without leave, & I don't think you need worry about leaving the boys in the middle. If you had been knocked out, you wouldn't have had any pangs.

"Swinging the lead" is an old-fashioned slang expression for shirking a duty, or taking time off work. Nothing could have been further from Bernard's nature. Nor Win's actually. But she was quite prepared to allow others to do so. Like him, she was determined to do her bit for the country, but she sounds unconvinced about the necessity for this war, a sentiment evidently shared by some of her patients.

"I am becoming quite a proficient lead-swinger," she declares, "through long and varied experience. A man came into

Win (SECOND FROM LEFT) at Beech House

my ward last August with a scalded foot; his foot was well in a couple of weeks & he is still going strong, & I have managed it quite alone. I have got quite a name for it amongst the patients, & how they all wish that I was the Captain who has to come round and mark them out. I wish I was too, because then the war would have ended long ago."

She would never have said such a thing in World War II, which to her was not just a conflict of nations or empires, but a struggle for survival.

Beech House seems to have been a happy experience on the whole. Even though it was a military hospital staffed by Jewish nurses, Christmas was celebrated with gusto: "We had such a jolly time. Matron was awfully sporting, & she let us smoke after the staff dinner on Christmas Day; or rather let me say that Matron and the Commandant were so absorbed in eating nuts and maintaining polite conversation, that they did not notice that the rest of us were filling the atmosphere with the pleasant perfume of Gold Flake cigarettes."

Well, she concludes, she hopes he will stay a long time at the Convalescent Camp in Alexandria: "Anyhow, here's the best of luck to you! All good wishes & Cheerio! from Winnie."

In fact, Bernard did not swing the lead at all, for just a few days after he wrote his letter from Alexandria, he was on the road to Jerusalem with General Allenby's army. There are, alas, no letters recording this event. He did sometimes mention it in conversations about Israel. Though he was never an ardent Zionist, entering the holy sites had evidently moved him.

The British prime minister, David Lloyd George, had insisted that the British take Jerusalem from the Turks by Christmas. Not that this would end the war any sooner, but it was hoped that such a feat would boost morale on the home front. Where even Richard Lionheart had failed in the Third Crusade in 1192, Lloyd George (or, more accurately, Allenby) had to succeed.

Passing along the same routes as the medieval Crusaders, past Hebron and the outskirts of Bethlehem, was not easy. British and Empire troops had to drag their artillery across foggy mountain passes on roads made almost impassable by incessant rainstorms. Horses and limbers often got stuck in the sticky black mud.

Allenby's aim was to surround Jerusalem and force the Turks to surrender without having to fight in the holy city itself. On December 9, victory was his. Christians once again ruled over a sacred Muslim site, even though Allenby tactfully left the Mosque of Omar, located directly across from the Church of the Holy Sepulchre, under Muslim control. On the eleventh, Allenby entered Jerusalem's Old City on foot through the Jaffa Gate, to show his respect, and was met by guards representing England, Scotland, Wales, Ireland, France, India, and Italy. He noted that "the population received me well."

All I have to show for Bernard's presence at this historic event is another one of his relics, a small "Album Souvenir," entitled in English and French: *Entrance of the British and Allied Troops in Jerusalem*. Between covers of cypress wood, engraved with a picture of the sacred Muslim Dome of the Rock, are a collection of dried "flowers from the Holy Land" and photographs of the Turkish surrender and Allenby's official entrance.

They are rather dull pictures, many of them a little out of focus: of British soldiers milling around, waiting for the general to arrive; of the general, still on horseback, riding through the outskirts of the town, with citizens, shielded from the sun by black parasols, watching his entrance from their balconies; of Allenby reading a proclamation to a mass of Turkish soldiers wearing fezzes; of Allenby departing on horseback; of the Duke of Connaught, one of Queen Victoria's sons, handing out medals. All I know about the duke is that he later became governor-general of Canada and was reputed to have sported a tattoo down his spine of a fox hunt with the hunted creature's tail disappearing into its hole.

Bernard was there. What he did exactly, how long he was there for, and what his movements were in the next few months,

I don't know. Regimental records mention the capture of Jericho in February and a number of scrappy fights in the Jordan Valley with a broken Ottoman enemy.

A letter dated May 24, 1918, does not give much more information. It is the first one addressed directly to "Dear Winnie" since the breakup in 1916. He writes:

> Fate has been having a game with me & knowing
> my peculiar attitude towards tramping, studied this pet
> aversion of mine & so ordained that I should join a
> distinctly mobile Division. Ever since we left the desert
> we have been—well, like my mother crossing Oxford
> Circus. Hither and thither and back again, regular fidgets
> until they have termed us the Cook's Tourists & our
> motto has become "Quo Vadis."

But quite where he was, away from the desert, is unclear. Records do show that his division was gradually being "Indianised"; that is to say, fresh troops from the Indian army were brought in to replace British soldiers, most of whom were sent back to France, Bernard evidently among them. For his next letter, of July 20, mentions that "they had to have us back here after all to put a different light on affairs, tho' ours is only a moral support as yet." He was probably in a dreary railway town close to Calais, named Audruicq, which had been turned into a massive munitions dump.

Bernard's battalion in France was joined by a number of men who had been on leave in England. He writes, "They are at once surrounded by numerous friends who clamour for news as to the condition of the really one and only country. All accounts are entirely satisfactory & tho' my leave has still got twelve weeks to wait, well, I am licking my lips."

Bernard was shipped back to England in October. The war was not yet quite over. The remnants of his regiment had moved farther into Flanders. Blood-soaked old battlegrounds— Ypres, Cambrai, Bapaume, Passchendaele—were finally taken by Allied troops. Even the once impregnable cliffs of Doiran in Macedonia had fallen to the Allies in September. The England that Bernard had left behind in 1916 was still feverish with patriotism. He returned to a country exhausted, financially drained, and sick of war. More than nine hundred thousand men from Britain and its empire had been lost. (France had lost more than a million, as had Russia and Austria-Hungary, and Germany almost two million.) But all this misery was eclipsed in family memory by a story recounted to us many times as a kind of miracle.

Bernard came back in relatively good shape, but he suffered from a sufficiently serious outbreak of boils that he was sent to a military hospital in London. By sheer coincidence he had landed not only in Beech House but in the exact ward where Win was nursing. She first realized that he was there by finding a photograph of herself in a laundry basket. It must have fallen out of a pocket in his tunic. Their love was instantly, if still rather secretly, rekindled. Bernard's boils must have been hard to get rid of, for he was still in hospital on November 11, when the war was finally over. His discharge from the army, dated January 1, 1919, still has his regimental address as Beech House Military Hospital, Brondesbury, London.

Like countless people all over the world, Win caught influenza, the disease that would kill more than fifty million in 1918, more than three times the number of dead in World War I. In her forced absence from Beech House, she wrote a letter to Bernard recommending, a little flippantly, that he should take a course in "Pelmanism" to face his difficulties in returning to civilian life. Pelmanism, named after the Pelman Institute, which offered a correspondence course in this mental technique, devised in the 1890s, was supposed to expand the mind and minimize inefficiency. Early fans included Sir Robert Baden-Powell, the Boy Scout leader, and Jerome K. Jerome, the author of *Three Men in a Boat*. Pelmanism is no longer in favour in psychiatric circles.

On November 3, Winnie thanks Bernard for lending her his copy of *My Lady Nicotine*, a novel by James Barrie about a middle-aged bachelor trying to give up smoking. She also mentions his boils, asking him whether he has any dressing on them, and hoping that he will still have a tiny boil left so he can remain in hospital long enough for her return to the ward and celebrate his birthday on the twenty-third.

In fact, he seems to have been well enough to leave the hospital to go to concerts, for Winnie asks him about a performance by the pianist Vladimir von Pachmann (the "von" was added by this Odessa-born Jewish musician himself).

The tone of the correspondence is still a little formal ("Dear Bernard, Thank you so much for your cheery letter . . ."), but their love was openly expressed. In the envelope of the letter Winnie sent on November 3, I found a lock of her brown hair, which looked as fresh as it was in 1918. Since I knew her only with thick grey hair, this discovery gave me an uncanny feeling, as though part of her had suddenly sprung back to physical life. I did not care to look at it, let alone touch it, for long.

Three days later, on November 6, Bernard sends her a copy of *Many Inventions*, a collection of short stories by another favourite author, Rudyard Kipling. He ends it with, "Cheery-oh, buck up & oust the 'flu, Bernard."

Her letter dated January 3, four days before his formal discharge from the army, is still addressed to "Dear Bernard," but she asks him whether he can come with her to a dance on the tenth. If he could, would he come and dine at 17 Parsifal Road first, and "have your clothes brought here as before."

There is a handwritten dance programme, dated March 18. Inside are fourteen dances, foxtrots, waltzes, and one-steps. Every dance has the initials of a booked partner. B.E.S. takes up five of the fourteen dances. He is by then a medical student at Emmanuel College, Cambridge, trying to make up for lost time. In a letter from "Emmers," dated May 1, he asks her for her photograph to keep in his wallet, and ends his letter with "Love from Bernard—It's nice to be able to say this without camouflage now."

Win's next letter, sent on June 30, begins, "Dear Boss-to-be, (You're not there yet tho', so don't start crowing too soon)." She recounts their first meeting, and how proud she was, a sixteen-year-old girl with her hair all the way down her back, of "the big jolly schoolboy who was head of his House." It was "ripping" of him, she continues, to write to her on Peace Night, June 28, when the Versailles Treaty was signed.

She adds, "It is the first great occasion that we have not

been together since you came home in September—and it was a great occasion for both of us, Bernard, apart from the general good. First—the League of Nations—which means that you will never never have to leave me to fight and endanger your life in any rotten war that can ever be invented. Second, that the two countries to which we both owe all we have, are no longer enemies."

Three

THE LONG WAIT

———·———

Bernard might have been drinking when he started this letter to Win. He is not sure about the date: "Somewhere between 20–30 of Jan., 1920," it says. "Saturday evening anyhow." The writing in blue ink on the top of the letter sent from Emmanuel College, Cambridge, looks distinctly uneven. It was in fact the twenty-sixth of January.

He starts off with an obscure reference to a music hall show featuring a bawdy cleaning lady called "Winnie." The letter resumes the next day, written in a darker type of ink. Bernard describes a late-night discussion with fellow students about the reasons why people choose certain careers. One man, he writes, maintained that such choices are based on one of three things: the chance of success, of making a great deal of money, or because your father was in the same line of work before you. None of these reasons motivated Bernard.

He writes, "I took up medicine to begin with primarily be-

cause I realised structurally how wonderful life is & then the
idea to be a doctor grew on me for quite a different reason.
Perhaps it was the war. It was there I saw anyway a man's gratitude for that little best you can do for him, when he is down
and under, however small it may be, and I decided that there is
nothing greater, nothing that can give one more satisfaction
than cheering up misery and helping the sick and wounded.
My job in life should be a doctor and his work—well, my religion. That is what I determined and I hope I shall carry it out.
There, that's enough of my soul even to you for one day. I've
never given word to these sentiments to anybody, hardly to
myself."

Win's reply to "Dear Bernie" starts off with a mention of a
forthcoming dance at the Schwabs', which promises to be "topping." She is also frightfully "bucked," because her cousin in
Kassel, the famous Jewish philosopher Franz Rosenzweig, has
finally become engaged to the girl he was about to propose to
six years before. This had been aborted then because, according to Win, "I turned up" and "quite inadvertently & quite un-
consciously messed their lives up for them, only temporarily
tho', thank goodness." Franz Rosenzweig had fallen in love
with Win.

I have good reason to be thankful that nothing came of it.
Franz was the only child of Georg Rosenzweig and Win's aunt,
Adele Alsberg, known to her as Tante Dele. Unsuited for any
combat role, Franz had served during the war as a spotter in an
anti-aircraft battalion in the Balkans and then, in 1917, in
Macedonia, facing Bernard, who was just a few miles away on
the other side. Apart from spotting enemy planes, Franz

lectured the troops on such topics as the meaning of Islam. His marriage, Win relates, meant so much to Tante Dele, more even than to most mothers, "because Franz is the only thing she has got in the world, & being a genius, he has always been a queer, restless, eccentric spirit, and very difficult and estranged sometimes." But "now that he has anchored, and has come home to roost at last," all would be well.

I have a small picture at home of Franz Rosenzweig as a toddler, being hugged closely, as though he might be snatched away at any moment, by a pretty-looking Tante Dele. The photograph was taken in Kassel at the studio of a Mr. Hegel.

Win could not have known that a year later, after publishing his best-known book, *The Star of Redemption*, laying out his proposal for a new approach to Judaism, Rosenzweig would develop Lou Gehrig's disease. Almost totally paralyzed in the last years of his life, propped up in a special chair in a small Frankfurt apartment, he dictated his essays to his devoted wife, Edith, by blinking an eye when she hit on the right letter in the alphabet. Rosenzweig died in 1929. His last words, taken down by Edith, were, "And now it comes, the point of all points, which the Lord has truly revealed to me in my sleep, the point of all points for which there . . ." And that is where it ended. There was no more.

Win always had a somewhat strained relationship with the "fearfully highbrow" side of her German family. She had no romantic interest in Rosenzweig. It is in any case hard to see her fitting into his religious as well as philosophical milieu. On the other hand, she was a highly intelligent woman. Who is to say that if she had lived in Kassel or Frankfurt, instead of in

London, she might not have been less keen to demonstrate her interest in golf and horses and been as highbrow as her German cousins?

Near the end of her letter she finally comes to Bernard's late-night thoughts on his chosen "religion," that is to say, his devotion to a medical career.

She is glad that he let her "have a little peep at your soul the other day—one so rarely gets a glimpse of it, altho' I have learned to fathom quite a good bit of it now, without your telling me anything." She quite understands his point about human gratitude being the most priceless thing in the world. Of course, she writes, "I experienced a bit of it too, altho' one cannot compare the sort of work I did during the war with what you boys did for each other out there, and what doctors do all their lives."

These were uneasy times. The worldwide flu epidemic was still raging. Bernard had seen enough horror in the war to be severely shaken. And yet there is not a hint of trauma in his letters, nor was there in his later life. The war had certainly affected him, hence his lifelong silence about his experiences. But if there was any trauma, he kept it well hidden.

Not everyone was so lucky. Win mentions, on February 9, 1920, a family friend named Stanley, who was "terribly, dangerously ill" with flu. He was delirious for four days and barely able to recognize his wife. It took two people to hold him in bed. When Win went to see him, Stanley "was shouting the whole place down. He is in a terrible rage nearly all the time and seems to be living through the whole war again."

Like most students of his generation, Bernard couldn't afford to waste time at university. Having lost four years to the war, he had to get on with it. And Bernard and Win officially announced their engagement on August 1, 1922. The announcement in *The Times*, kept with their letters, is stuck to the paper from a press clipping bureau. It is part of a bundle of letters of congratulations from family and friends tied neatly together with a piece of string. Almost every one comes from an address within twenty minutes' walk of Finchley Road station in Hampstead. However, they couldn't afford to actually get married until Bernard had completed his studies and hospital training and found a suitable job. This meant years of waiting, longing, pining for the day, until they were finally wed in 1925. The question was what she would do in the meantime. And the way they behaved to each other in those seemingly endless three years of waiting is scarcely imaginable today.

Bernard's views on women's proper role in life, although far from radical, sometimes seemed to be more progressive than Win's. But then her opinions were often coloured by a chronic lack of self-confidence. In a letter, still addressed to "Dear Bernard," on July 26, 1919, Win writes that her parents "are such dears" that they might allow her to study at Oxford, even though "it would be a great sacrifice to them." But she doesn't want to go: "I feel it is my place, now that I am grown up, to be at home and help Mother . . . In any case, Oxford would be a tremendous luxury, which is not at all necessary, just at present of all times. I should have a very bad conscience about accepting it."

She wrote this almost a year after British women had been given the right to vote in an Act of Parliament. The war had changed the lives of women forever, since they had been mobi-

lized to work on the home front while the men were dying on
the Continent. Even comfortably well-off women like Win
could no longer be pushed back into the purely domestic roles
they had been stuck with in the past.

Bernard's response to Win's letter, though phrased with the
slight condescension that was customary, is encouraging:
"About Oxford, Winnie dear, I really don't quite know what to
say. I am still in favour of it, really, if you are spareable . . .
Oxford will give you firstly occupation for your thoughts, brain
and mind in the form of friends and whatever subjects of interest to you that you take up, and secondly occupation for your
body in fresh air and exercise; and these are two of the essential of several ingredients in the recipe of a contented and
happy Winnie or anyone else in your position."

A year later, in a letter addressed to "My darling, adorable
little girl," Bernard finds the perfect expression of his views on
modern women in a short item he had cut out from the newspaper. "I enclose, Win, an extraordinarily good cutting from
the *Sunday Times*," he writes on November 7, 1921. "It bucked
me up no end when I read it as it epitomises exactly what I
want to say and think in a few terse well chosen sentences."

They are the words of a Miss E. Wordsworth, of Lady Margaret Hall, Oxford, who had just received a degree of M.A.
honoris causa. She writes, "I hope the words 'sex-antagonism'
will never be breathed in our Oxford air. I should like to take
this opportunity of reminding our younger students that, when
all is said and done, the best contribution any woman can make
to the world is her womanliness, and that if she loses that the
life of humanity will be far more impoverished than it could

possibly be enriched by her passing any number of examinations or holding her own with the most erudite of professors."

Bernard's comment: "Take it to heart, all ye modern girls. You have, I know darling, and that is one of the many reasons why I love you."

In fact, Oxford was rather more hospitable to female students than Cambridge at the time. In a letter dated November 30, 1919, Bernard remarks in passing, "You will look funny in cap and gown. I see girls at Oxford can now take degrees there and will wear gowns at leccers [lectures] like the men. The first step towards emancipation of women up there."

It is clear that he approved of this. Despite his fairly conventional views on the female sex, he was not a chauvinist. In a letter sent on February 1, 1920, Bernard writes about attending a concert at the Cambridge Musical Club with a programme that was "too modern for my taste," even though he liked the Elgar Violin Sonata. Then he observes, "The admittance of members of Newnham and Girton* into the C.M.C. was defeated by 1 vote . . . so you see Cambridge are just as bad in some ways as Oxford as regards women."

Win was in most things more conservative than Bernard, certainly when it came to politics. She was not a "feminist" in the modern sense of the term, but neither was she happy with female subservience. Win frequently wished that she were a man. After a visit to Oxford in February 1919 to see her elder brother, Walter, act in a student production with his contemporary at university, John Gielgud, she writes, "You know, men

---

*Both are women's colleges established in the latter half of the nineteenth century.

do have a good time up at the 'Varsity—it strikes me anew every time I go to Oxford or Cambridge. I would give anything to be a man just for the sake of Public School or 'Varsity; it's all so different from a girl's career, & I should love to take some magic potion & transform myself."

The same sentiment is repeated in November of that year, again after a visit to her brother at Oxford: "I should simply adore to be reincarnated a man & go either to Christ Church or Magdalen . . . however, it is too late now."

And so she frets all through 1919 and 1920, feeling duty-bound to stay at home in Parsifal Road, working on her matriculation from school and looking after her parents, even as she knows that "it would make a lot of difference to me to get away from here for a bit to quite other surroundings. I have never been away from home in my life . . . You see I have got your future to consider too, Bun, & I have got to keep as young and fresh as I can . . . but with this kind of life for another four or five years I should just stagnate. But it seems so selfish to try and get away . . . I wish I knew what I ought to do. I have been revolving it round and round in my mind and I can't come to any conclusion." This is on June 7, 1920.

In a letter written earlier in that same year, she apologizes for going on about inconsequential things: "I suppose it is really because I lead such a newsless existence, there is nothing else to write about—one continuous unbroken round of [reading] *The Times*, food, mathematics, Latin, Greek, fiddle, massage, exercise, *Times* & so on ad infinitum, none of them particularly interesting topics upon which to enlarge."

There were some diversions, apart from visiting Walter at Oxford. Evenings at the Everyman Theatre in Hampstead—"so very embarrassingly gemütlich," because one was always running into people one knows—where she saw George Bernard Shaw's *Pygmalion*: "He was sitting in the 2d row & laughed heartily at his own jokes." Then there was Gilbert and Sullivan's *Mikado*: "I came away so delighted and refreshed . . . I believe that if I had the choice of Grand Opera, any play going, or Gilbert and Sullivan, I should choose the latter." She played the violin in an outfit called Grünebaum's Opera School Orchestra. In October 1919, she is about to lead the Fauré Quartet: "I am awfully funky, because I have never seen nor heard the thing, and I shall not have a second to practice it as I am going away over the weekend—moreover it is modern—& you know what that means."

Modernity is of course a relative concept. I was once told by my great-uncle Walter that his parents couldn't abide Brahms. They thought his music was just noise. Win assures Bernard in a letter of February 4, 1920, that if he listens often enough, he will "come to appreciate the comprehensible of the modern music, César Franck, Debussy & Chausson. You know Walter was a confirmed anti-any-music-later-than-Mozart man until quite recently, and now he suddenly revels in Brahms."

Brahms, as I mentioned earlier, was one of Win and Bernard's shared passions, as much as if not more so than the plays and books of James Barrie. They adored Wagner as well, but Brahms, Win writes, "always wins to this day with me. He has such a limpid, flowing rhythm, and such marvellously blended harmonies, like a sort of iridescent opalescent colouring. I don't know whether you can translate music into colours, I can't generally, but Brahms always produces that effect on me. His music is so essentially pure with very rarely any passion in it, it just dreams away like a rippling brook, very beautifully."

Perhaps Bernard's response reflects a more worldly understanding of human passion. To "Dearest little girl," he writes on February 8, "I don't entirely agree with you about Brahms . . . I don't think he is always the bland, dreamy sort of man you want to make out. I have on many occasions seen his face quite flushed, his pulse quicken, his veins stand out on his head, his lips quiver as they poured out some story of love."

About physical passion, Bernard, though still inexperienced, was a good deal less innocent than she was. There was during their long years of waiting a great deal of cuddling and kissing. On September 27, 1920, Win writes to "My angel" that he should close his eyes and "pretend I am as close to you as it is possible to be, and that I am giving you the longest kiss you have ever had in your life. Then, when it is all over, we both sigh rapturously and start all over again."

Bernard ends most of his letters with such sentiments as these (August 8, 1920):

> Darling Win, come and sit on my knee & let me
> stroke and cover you with kisses all over and thereby
> show you in some small way how I love you,
>> My eternal love
>> from your very own Bun

When Win invites him to an "At Home" at Parsifal Road with dancing to commence at 8:30, she scribbles a note that a "discreet sitting out place" might be in the offing in an airing cupboard on the second floor of the house.

Still, I am convinced that things did not go further than that. Two incidents seem to bear this out. In March 1920, Win went up to Cambridge to visit Bernard. It was evidently an idyllic weekend, with breakfasts ("brekkers") and dances, to which unmarried female partners often came with a chaperone, so nothing untoward could happen. Quite what Bernard said to Win at one of these dances is not spelled out, perhaps something about indecent pictures he might have seen in Egypt during the war. Whatever it was, she was shaken by the experience. Here is her response, on March 17, to "Bern, my one and only love":

> I'm afraid you must have thought I was very stupid & prudish the other day—but what you told me at the dance just gave me a bit of a shock at first. I always imagined, as far as I ever considered the subject at all, that that type of picture was supplied just for one type of man, and not a very desirable type, and that your type loathed it and was repulsed by it just as much as I was— and so at first I was a little shocked and self-conscious, like I was when I first heard about all the relations between man and woman, but once I have assimilated these ideas and got used to them, it's quite alright. Men are just fundamentally different from women. They have different feelings and conceptions and a totally different

outlook on life . . . You see I am very proud of my sex, and of the honour of my sex, and it seemed to me that that kind of picture must debase us, and that once a man has seen a woman so stripped of all modesty, even if it is only a picture of one, the whole sex must sink in his eyes and be held lightly by him for evermore.

This was not an unreasonable response to pornography. It was even one that many feminists of later generations, rightly or wrongly, would have endorsed. It doesn't even mean necessarily that her physical relations with Bernard didn't exceed kisses in discreet alcoves. But there was another incident in February 1921, when he evidently tried to "go too far." His letter, sent from Emmanuel College on the twelfth, is full of contrition: "My adored Win, my rock of life," it begins:

You are a little brick. It's a very humble shame-faced, hang-headed Bun that's writing to you now. I always told you I wasn't worthy even to lick your shoes and now I have unwillingly proved it.

You <u>thought</u> we were doing wrong, that even engaged people are not allowed to pretend they are married. <u>I</u> <u>knew</u> it all along & yet singly I was too weak to battle against it.

I used to go away, make wonderful resolutions, come back and break them, & so life went on. I wanted to speak about it, so that we could join hands, for I felt that you were fighting just the same. Then I remembered once when I had said something at Cambridge, and you got so unhappy and blamed your innocent self & tried to cast

yourself down in my estimation, when all the time it was
this worthless fellow. I think one could almost call oneself
a cad in this instance for most men should know & I do
know that altho' a man is most easily excitable, woman is
harder to become excited, but once excited, her inhibiting
powers are even less than a man's. Win, darling, you are
the good woman for having put a stop to it and I the bad
man for having let it go on.

Win's reply, given the conventions of the time, is loving and
generous. She thanks him for his understanding: "My dearest,
it was certainly not your fault; it has always been man's privilege to be weak in those things, just as it has for ever been
woman's duty to be strong. You simply accepted your privilege,
while I failed lamentably in my duty, so it is I who come to you
and ask your forgiveness, my dear one." She goes on to say how
much stronger their marital bonds will be for "fighting our
battles together."

This is the same letter in which she laments not being a
man. She was referring to men's pleasures in university life. But
there could be another way of reading this sentiment. She
might, consciously or not, have tired, at least once in a while, of
her duty to be strong.

To fight against sexual temptation was for most people,
especially of their background, the norm. Bernard was surely
right when he said, less in his own defence than as a statement
of fact, that his friskiness was "one of the natural results of a
very lengthy engagement." The physical longing that must have
tormented both of them is beyond the imagination of men and

women grown up after the middle of the twentieth century, for whom delayed gratification is merely a waste of time. But this may not be in every respect a gain. The passion felt by Win and Bernard is perhaps equally beyond the comprehension of those who have never experienced such yearning.

In the end, after much dithering on her part and encouragement on his, Win did go to Oxford, to St. Hilda's Hall, founded in 1893 as a college for women. Among her letters is a large photograph, taken in 1924, of Win sitting with faculty and students in the senior common room. As one of the shortest people present, Win is seated in the second row, behind a number of taller women sitting on the ground. Nothing in her rather shy demeanour suggests that she was actually the president of the SCR. She has dark rings under her eyes, suggesting sleeplessness. The hairstyle of the time, thick mops of hair brushed back rather severely from the parting, and the college look of blue blazers and sensible sweaters, does not flatter the students lined up for the official photograph. They look distinctly dowdy.

That Win was the exact contemporary at Oxford of Evelyn Waugh and his circle of aesthetes seems extraordinary. They were worlds apart. While the Old Etonian dandies of Christ Church were hopping into one another's beds, declaiming modern poetry through megaphones, and rolling around drunk in the quad, Win and her friends were singing in choirs, punting on the river, and enjoying "cocoa evenings" in their rooms.

Still, something of the languid atmosphere of Oxford seeps into her letters once in a while, despite her innocence compared to the aesthetes. Here she is on "May Morning," the traditional revelry after all-night balls, when the new day is heralded by hymn-singing from the top of Magdalen Tower: "Upon the stroke of six from the Magdalen bell, there was a breathless hush, as instantly the melody broke forth upon the morning air, and floated down to us, clear and thin. The minute the hymns were over, there was a wild stampede of punts, canoes, scullers, each making tracks for a coveted breakfast spot . . . The river was crowded and it was like a summer's day, everybody in flannels and bright clothes. We looked a disgrace and behaved very badly—sucking oranges through sugar in the face of the public and smoking, which is strictly forbidden" (May 5, 1922).

Win read modern languages, but concentrated on German literature rather than French. She must already have been reasonably fluent in German when she chose that subject for her school exams, along with classics and maths. Apart from a fondness for reading stories to us from *Struwwelpeter* (*Shock-headed Peter*) when we were children, which we enjoyed, and the plots of Wagner's operas, which we didn't, she never showed a particular devotion to German literature, so far as I can remember. But she does mention, in a letter written on October 19, 1919, that she was "working up" one of two "stiff books" for her examinations. She chose Heinrich Heine's *Zur Geschichte der Religion und Philosophie in Deutschland* (*Religion and Philosophy in Germany*), a "hefty work," she declares, "but awfully interesting."

Win's relationship with Germany and the German lan-

May Ball

guage was ambivalent, as one might expect. As long as I knew her, she always expressed a healthy British disdain for the native country of her parents. The first German expression I became aware of, I think, was *Schadenfreude*, taking pleasure in the misfortune of others, something Win described to us many times as a particularly German characteristic.

Children from mixed marriages or children of immigrants seldom adopt an attitude of complete cultural neutrality. It is easier now that mixed marriages in many Western cities are becoming the norm rather than the exception. But people in previous generations often felt the need to choose, and would identify with one half of their "identity" by excessively disparaging the other. In the case of Bernard and Win, Germany's behaviour made it rather easy for them to plump wholeheartedly for the country of their birth. My own life owes a great deal to their choices, since my often rosy-hued view of England was to some degree a caricature of theirs—a caricature of a caricature, really.

The fiercely anti-German sentiments of the British had not disappeared just a few years after the war. Yet Win's correspondence still sends mixed signals. In August 1920, she was spending a holiday with her parents and her sister, Margaret (Meg), at a hotel on the coast of Devon. She eyes the empty dance floor wistfully and is reminded of Bernard's absence. With him, or any man, in the party, she thinks that "we should soon get to know other people, but Margaret and I alone never will, I fear. Mother and father are naturally rather shy and retiring people and more so under present circumstances." These circumstances clearly had nothing to do with being Jewish and everything with having German accents.

In late October of that same year, however, she is astonished at how much German is spoken in a play by John Galsworthy, set in an Austrian railway station. "They couldn't have done that a year or so back," she remarks. The play she saw, entitled *The Little Man*, was in fact written in 1913. The theme is practical altruism, as opposed to the merely verbal kind. Win sees the play chiefly as a study of national characteristics: the noisy, verbose Yank, the doltish Dutch boy, the English exchanging discreet smiles at the foolishness of foreigners, and the German, "who is pompous, overbearing and selfish."

Win was less sentimental about "family" than Bernard; she was indeed less sentimental about everything, except for her devotion to him, which I hesitate to call sentimental. Family visits to Kassel were regarded as a duty rather than as a pleasure. But her account of a visit in July 1920 to Uncle Adolf Alsberg, a well-to-do surgeon who worked on X-rays with the famous Dr. Röntgen, Cousin Franz the philosopher, Tante Dele, and others is fascinating on many levels.

This was only two years after the most devastating war in the history of man. She is delighted to see that German officials have become much friendlier than before the war, to the point of being almost obsequious: bags are checked only casually and with a smile, stationmasters see to the foreign traveller's every comfort. British soldiers, still stationed in the occupied Rhineland, wave them through passport control, "perhaps because we were countrymen of theirs."

When Win and her brother, Walter, arrive in Kassel, they are immediately "surrounded and slobbered over by seething masses of relatives." Walter, not normally a placid man, is behaving "like a lamb," and although "some of the people are far from tactful in their remarks, he and I are taking it all philosophically and smothering our sentiments. After all it is only a fortnight, and we are being as quiet and amiable and affectionate as good little nieces and nephews should be."

As to the possible nature of these remarks, and Walter's response to them, I shall come to that presently.

In spite of some obvious hardships due to the past war, such as an acute shortage of coal, so that even prosperous families such as the Alsbergs in Kassel can have hot baths only twice a week, Win is stunned by the elegance and comfort of their lives. The food is excellent, "Onkel" Adolf's house is "palatial," fitted with every modern appliance and exquisitely furnished with "a glorious collection of pictures and antique furniture and marvellously blended carpets." Ah, she exclaims, "People here do understand real comfort . . . far better than they do in England."

Standing on the balcony of this palatial house, Win gazes at the "glorious countryside" with the "ex-Kaiser's 'Schloss' bang in the centre of the view,"* and she is struck by the "bitter irony" that "six years of such stirring disaster could pass over the world and yet leave all this just as it was, lying there so serenely, and peacefully, and we here just the same as ever, gazing at it all, and the old Schloss smiling at us in the same old way, although it has changed hands now. I am thankful that nature can withstand so much, aren't you?"

This was on July 7, 1920. After 1945, the Schloss, Uncle Adolf's house, and most of Kassel had been flattened by bombs, and none of the relatives who stayed in Germany had survived Hitler's Reich; a large and hideous property company stands on the spot of the house today.

On July 11, Win's tone changes sharply. "My own beloved," she begins, "I am so home-sick for you, and I haven't had a single syllable to comfort me." She is "longing for England again, although [the relatives] are all fearfully good to us here." Then comes a familiar complaint: "They are so horribly brainy, and I can't follow them in all their intellectual flights, philosophical, literary, and religious . . . I thank heaven daily that you are not one of these genii with an abnormal portion of grey

---

*She is referring to the castle called Wilhelmshöhe, where the kaiser spent his summers between 1899 and 1918. At the end of World War I, the castle was used by Field Marshal von Hindenburg when he demobilized the German army. Reconstruction started in 1968.

matter, but that you are a normal, cheerful, warm-hearted man with a sense of humour and human understanding. These people are all in the first place philosophers and 'Gelehrter' [scholars] and in second place human beings and family men, and they are all so earnest—they hardly know how to laugh and they can't take life lightly."

Having struggled myself with the highly abstract language of Franz Rosenzweig's theological works, I can see why Win grew a little impatient. I also recognize her sentiments in those of her eldest son, my uncle John, the film director. This highly educated man (Balliol College, Oxford) was always going on about "intellectuals," as though they were enemies trying to oppress him or make him feel inferior. I was an "intellectual" in his eyes, and forgiven for this flaw only because I was his nephew. But this attitude had more to do with his artistic temperament. He stressed his instinctive qualities, which were, in his defensive view, beyond the understanding of critics and others who lived by their intellect. In Win's case, something else was at play, something directly related to her idea of being English. For it is an old patriotic prejudice, going back at least to the eighteenth century, that the true son of Roast Beef and Old England is blessed with instinctive common sense, a humorous disposition, and human decency, while the Frenchman is affected and the German abstract and ponderous.

Her brother, Walter, was always regarded as the highbrow in the family. My mother was rather afraid of him, worried that some intellectual insufficiency on her part would be exposed. Some of her brothers and sisters felt rather the same. My uncle

Roger in particular, the cricketer in the family, was disapproved of as a sportsman, and thus a bit of a philistine.

I liked Uncle Walter (I never called him "Great-Uncle"), a barrister and judge by profession. We would have earnest conversations in the kitchen of his house in Hampstead, in the street where Sigmund Freud once lived, about God and the meaning of life, while his wife, Aunty Dora, was in the living room with her female companion. Uncle Walter's own sexual proclivities were ambiguous and probably never acted upon; he did have a lifelong penchant for work with troubled youths, and was reputed to show a certain leniency in court towards handsome young men. Walter and Dora produced six children. It was an eccentric household.

On their visit to Kassel in 1920, there clearly had been an unpleasant confrontation between Walter and his cousin Franz Rosenzweig, who was then busy setting up a centre for Jewish learning in Frankfurt. How to forge an authentic, unapologetic Jewish identity in the mainstream of German society was his life's work. This unsettled Walter, who had converted to Anglicanism just at the time when his cousin had resisted a similar temptation. The story I was always told is that Franz decided against such a move, even as he was about to step into a church. This is not actually what happened. He had indeed decided to become a Christian, in 1913, but he wanted to do so *as a Jew.* Like his British relatives, he grew up in a non-religious family who believed in assimilation. His closest friend was a Jew who had converted. So instead of stepping into a church, Franz first entered a synagogue in Berlin on Yom Kippur. That is when he decided that he would remain true to the faith of his ancestors after all. Unusually for a German Jew, Rosenzweig was much taken by the Polish Jews he had met during the war. They seemed happier in their skins, more genuine than middle-class German Jews, whom, in a letter to his mother, Franz called "degenerate parvenus."*

Referring to their unhappy encounter in Kassel, Walter sent a letter to Franz more or less apologizing for his hostility, but still accusing Franz of being humourless, too theoretical, and morbid. But a more extraordinary exchange followed three years later, in November 1923, when Walter explained why he became a Christian and a socialist. He believed that only the universal spirit of Christ would finally do away with racial, religious, and national divisions. This line of thinking was not entirely original. There were many Jews who thought that Marxism would perform the same miracle. With Walter's letter came a long essay, which managed to be both facile and pompous. It is entitled 'The Jews'.

It is in this essay that some of Win's sentiments about the family in Kassel are most clearly echoed, albeit in a somewhat more robust fashion. "The Englishman," Uncle Walter intones, "takes his cold dip in the early morning, when the hoar-frost glitters on the lawns, plays his game of football in the blinding rain, and stands half the day in the deep field, roasting in the sun, just waiting to stop a cricket ball; and the Jew, with a self-satisfied shrug of his shoulders, sits at his office desk and

---

*Franz Rosenzweig: His Life and Thought, presented by Nahum N. Glatzer (New York: Schocken, 1961).

smiles—'Let them do it,' he thinks, 'if it amuses them; personally I am much better employed here and infinitely more comfortable.'"

It is possible that a certain irony is intended here, which
would almost surely have been lost on Rosenzweig. But I'm not
sure irony was Walter's strong suit either. He continues, "But
perhaps he [the Jew] is wrong . . . even today the mingy little
man loses in personality what he gains in intellect; and while the
brainless giant may be a pompous ass, the self-assertive dwarf is
as often considered a bumptious little worm. And that is pre-
cisely what we, alas, too easily become, when we allow the spirit
excessive liberties with the flesh."

These are astonishing words, coming from a man who
never voluntarily stopped a cricket ball in his life—indeed, one
of the family legends, conveyed to me by my mother, was that
"ball play was forbidden in Uncle Walter's house."

He goes on, lecturing his brilliant German cousin: "Those
of us who have been to an English Public School or have served
in the Great War, have begun to realise this, for we have been
taught to develop body and mind in their right proportions,
and have at least had the opportunity of seeing and appreciat-
ing the other point of view."

In Walter's case appreciation turned into complete assimilation. It was time, he argued, to discard the "mad, antiquated
and unworthy" Jewish belief in their status as the chosen ones
and melt into the bosom of Christ.

Rosenzweig dictated an exquisitely polite riposte, dated
December 28, 1923. He was not at all surprised to hear about
the turn his cousin's life had taken. That was on the cards ever

since his parents decided to send him to an English boarding school. Had he converted with an eye on worldly advantage? Not consciously, to be sure. "However," writes Franz, "that there are certain advantages which you will hardly be able to avoid, is beyond question."

As far as Walter's essay on the Jews is concerned, Franz strongly advises him not to publish it. In his words, "Jews have every right to criticize Jewishness harshly. And Christians can be as stupid about Judaism as they like. But a Jew who gets baptized cannot be in either camp. For on this topic, no one will believe him."

Walter's mother, my great-grandmother Anna Alsberg, whom I can just about remember as a kindly old lady who served us high tea in her flat in St. John's Wood and spoke English with an accent, followed her son into the Anglican Church.

Win did not. She resisted any organized faith, even though in the last years of her life she regularly accompanied Bernard to the Liberal* Jewish synagogue in Oxford. As a young woman she slightly disapproved of Bernard's residual loyalty to the religion he had been brought up in. There is a humorous reference to their differences in a letter sent on September 21, 1920, by Bernard from the Regina Palace Hotel in Switzerland, where he was on holiday with his parents. Holidays abroad were taken quite regularly by the Schlesinger family, mostly in Switzer-

---

*What is called the Liberal synagogue in Britain is known as Reform in the United States.

land, a country of which Bernard would remain deeply fond for the rest of his life.

He thanks Win for sending them a tin of proper English tea: "You saved our lives with it as the Swiss stuff is no better than hay." He then announces that he will be fasting on the following day—"Day of Atonement, you know." She might well not have known. He continues, "Watch her disapproving face! Still, I am ready to uphold my personal view to the whole Regensburg family severally, or collectively . . . Never mind, Win, in future years when I've trolled off to one of my yearly visits to Synagogue and have sent you off with a friend to get a square meal somewhere, I won't forget to put in a good word for you."

The question of religion would crop up many times in their correspondence. But the most dramatic instance of her doubts and his liberal composure is an exchange in October 1920, a few months after her visit to Kassel. It deserves to be quoted at some length, as it tells us a lot not only about Bernard and Win but also about many people who shared a similar background, not only in England, of course.

Win had seen a religious play in London called *The Unknown*, which had unsettled her, since it brought up "the problem of the discord which springs up between those who have faith and those who do not, however much they may love each other."

"Dearest," she writes, "it is a tough problem, and as neither of us have faith or any real religion in our hearts, it is very very hard to bring up our children and give them the best."

They had evidently talked about this before, and her first

inclination had been that she should take the children to synagogue every week and raise them as Jews. But, she says, that really "wouldn't do—it would be hypocritical; how could I instil into them a belief that is wholly lacking in me? All orthodox religion is meaningless to me and leaves me cold, while public worship is even more repugnant to me." Still, she would be willing to "overcome all this and go to Synagogue every week for their sakes—if it would help, but it won't. They will ask me questions which I shall be unable to answer, because I cannot *feel* the answer, and so they will quickly find that I am cold and unconvincing and they will gain nothing."

Still, despite her misgivings, she is not an atheist. God, she believes, "is a natural instinct born into every human being, because he is a necessary supplement to human weakness." And so she predicts that their future children "will go to school and learn Christianity from those who have faith, and become Christians, and that will be the first breach between them and us."

She envies people who have faith: "If only either of us, or both of us could believe!" But she sees no point in picking up scraps of a religion, or taking their future offspring to synagogue "once or twice a year and make them fast 'just to remind them they are Jews,' and thereby deliberately do them out of gaining a faith, even though it is not our own."

Here was a dilemma that many educated secular Jews must have struggled with. Franz Rosenzweig's answer was to actively embrace Judaism, not as a religious doctrine or an organized faith, but as a form of acceptance, not accorded by others, but of oneself. In his words, "Nothing more is assumed than the simple resolve to say once: 'Nothing Jewish is alien to me.'"

This was a step that neither Win, nor Bernard, nor perhaps most people of their class and time were able or willing to take. It would be absurd to blame them, even if, as with all choices in life, this too came with a price, perhaps more keenly felt by Win than by Bernard, whose own response was a little closer to Rosenzweig's.

In his answer to Win's letter, dated October 18, 1920, he tells her not to worry so much. First of all, her anxiety is premature. Besides, no one knows all the answers to religious questions; people just believe, that is all. Having to attend chapel once in a while at school didn't convert him, so it shouldn't necessarily affect their future children. The best thing parents can do for their children is to show them by example how to lead a good and charitable life. He too was against "pointless ceremonies." He made up his own prayers in synagogue and came away "feeling better." Keeping the Day of Atonement "is only a matter of policy on my part in which 'I tell the world,' as the Yank would say, that I am by birth a Jew, a Jew still and proud of it too."

Perhaps it was his greater self-confidence in this matter that made it simpler for Bernard to feel at ease in a wider world, a confidence that, paradoxically, might have been helped by a childhood lived in a religious culture he had abandoned. At least he knew what it was that he was leaving behind, which made him less self-conscious, not just in matters of faith. He would tell Win about the grandeur of the Swiss countryside, the fascination of the Middle East, or the wonders of France. He longed to share these enthusiasms with her. They would make her less insular, he hoped.

Her response, in a letter sent on September 8, 1920, to the Regina Palace Hotel, was entirely in character: "Switzerland must be wonderful and I can imagine the grandeur, even though I have never seen it, but although I know I should love that too, somehow the nice cosy English countryside appeals to me more . . . I am afraid I am a home bird and I am just pervaded with the spirit of England. Nothing in the wide world will ever surpass it for me."

This was not just a pretence. Win was pervaded with the spirit of England as much as anyone could be. But her particular background continued to be a source of anxiety. No matter how much she revelled in the Englishness of her surroundings, she could never shake a slight sense of unease, a fear of rejection, a self-consciousness not shared by her Gentile friends, or at least not for the same reasons.

Win's first letter from St. Hilda's College, Oxford, written on October 16, 1921, to "My most precious and passionately adored Bun," is a deeply unhappy one. She had never felt so homesick. She is "utterly forlorn and unhappy." Leaving home for Oxford was "like being wrenched out of Paradise and plunged into Purgatory . . . dumped all alone in this queer, confusing place." She lies awake at night, his wristwatch the only visible thing in the darkness—"I could have hugged it because it was yours."

Many students feel that way in the first few weeks or months. In her case, there was also that nagging anxiety, which appears to have been completely superfluous. The principal of the college, a Miss Winifred Moberly, who had the unusual experience of administering hospitals in Russia during the war, "asked me if I was Jewish, and then said I need not attend Chapel unless I liked to . . . and asked if I was particular about food. Awfully decent of her, don't you think?" Win decides to attend morning chapel anyway, since the others are compelled to do so, and she doesn't want to stand out. She ends her letter telling Bernard once more how miserable she feels: "Ever your worshipping wife to be, Win."

Attached in the same envelope is a short note, written at 7 p.m. on the same day. She is feeling much better now, after she has been invited to a tea party, and "the hockey captain is anxious for me to join and will coach me specially at odd hours in a neighbouring field. I must get a hockey stick sent down & a gym tunic made post haste."

For all the talk about "the English spirit," the cosiness of the English countryside, and the hockey sticks, soon to be joined by reports of rowing and punting, high teas, and cocoa parties, it is easy to forget that Win had spent much of her sheltered existence in a narrow Hampstead milieu of mostly German Jews. Her social life with the Schwabs, the Seligmans, and the Fernbergs would be replaced quite swiftly by friendships with people who had very different names. But the self-consciousness would remain.

Less than a fortnight after her first letter, Win tells Bernard about a new friend she has made in the college. "I have just gone through the terrifying ordeal of entertaining my friend, complete with her mother and a second year, to cocoa in my room . . . I have just heard tonight that my friend's father was a

Punting in Cambridge

parson before he moved on to higher climes—I wonder if she will get a bad shock when she hears one day that I'm a Jewess."

Shortly after that, on November 12, she wants Bernard to reassure his mother that she won't become a Christian at Oxford. Indeed, she has been invited to attend various "Jewish meetings" at New College and Merton—"Rather amusing, don't you think? I wonder if I should be the only female; I am certainly the only Jewess here, but nobody suspects me of it yet."

There is in fact no evidence in any of her letters that she ever encountered anti-Semitism at Oxford. Perhaps she was too proud to say so, if it did occur. But I don't think so. Bernard's story was slightly different, though not at Cambridge, where he was his gregarious self, playing rugger for his college's first XV, racing his father's Bentley on public roads, playing golf, and making new friends with such names as "Jumbo" Monteith. (Bernard's own nickname, going back to his school-days, was also Jumbo, due to his physical clumsiness; it was an odd sensation, as a child, to hear the delighted exclamation "Jumbo!" when my grandfather had been recognized in the street by some elderly gentleman.) Bernard's trouble began when he had to apply for a job at one of the London hospitals.

Certain hospitals were known to be inhospitable to Jews. This antipathy was seldom expressed directly, but couched in terms of the patients' interests; they might not like to be treated by someone who seemed a little foreign. Bernard didn't even try for a place in some of those hospitals. But he had a difficult time getting into the less prejudiced institutions too, racing around to get letters of recommendation, ingratiating himself with board members of this place and that. The Jewish question, in his accounts to Win, is always approached obliquely. To complain about it directly was beneath his dignity. Where it showed was in his remarkable, perhaps even excessive, loyalty to those institutions where he *was* accepted, such as the Royal Army Medical Corps, University College Hospital, where he did his medical training, and indeed, although it can hardly be called an institution, England.

In 1923 and 1924 he tried very hard to get a job at Great Ormond Street Hospital for Sick Children in London. Success would depend on several things, he wrote in a letter to Win on

February 28, 1923. One of them was "My name." Still, he wrote, "I feel in fine battling spirit and was pleased to find so many willing friends at Hospital."

When he was still without a job on April 3, 1924, he wrote, "Oh Hell, it's a rotten world and what an uncountable amount of time has been wasted tramping those accursed Harley and Wimpole Streets. Even my staunch maxims of 'that'll be alright' & 'it's all for the best' seem to me with my present jaundiced eye somewhat threadbare and one even begins to wonder if it really will be alright in the end." But he concludes the letter by saying he will "put on a stout front . . . They say a Jew will worm his way in through a keyhole & so by Gad this one is going to get into Gt. Ormond Street some time or die in the attempt."

Finally, in 1927, he did get a position at Great Ormond Street, though not yet a permanent one, after what Win described in a letter to her parents as "a fearfully close contest. And only a series of lucky events helped Bun to win it in the end, in spite of an anti-Semitic intrigue amongst a large section of the staff."

"The name"—that is as close as he gets to naming anti-Semitism. Much later, in 1938, after failing to get a position at St. Thomas's Hospital in London, he writes, "45 [the family code meaning Jewish]—the old, old story." But that was it. Sly social snubs, which must have occurred more than once, were regarded as nuisances too vulgar to pay any attention to. I don't believe that Bernard was ever bothered by the high anxiety that plagued Win. But it is too easy to forget, when reading their letters, that prejudice against Jews, however mild or strictly social, was still the norm in the world that Bernard and Win tried so hard to make their own.

Meanwhile, the years go by, those long years of yearning and pining. Without Bernard passing his medical exams at Cambridge and landing a hospital job, they still couldn't get married. On December 4, 1923, Win writes, "The patience of the extra waiting would not matter, the only sad thing is that youth is so fast slipping away." Bernard visits Oxford and Win Cambridge, but they can rarely be alone. A "river party" in Oxford is cancelled (Win to Bernard, May 9, 1922), because Miss Moberly, the principal, "insisted on a chaperone and asked of whom exactly the party consisted. I thereupon had to explain your identity, thinking that must instantly solve the problem, as all engaged people here go about from morning till night with their affiancéds, but she loathes people being engaged . . . and still insisted on a chaperone." A walking tour in the country is planned for the spring of 1923, after they had already been formally engaged for a year, but that too has to be in the company of others, since, as Win writes, "unfortunately a walking tour for us two alone couldn't be done before we are married."

While waiting for that day, "ill with longing," she sends him letters overflowing with tender sentiments, kissing his lips "daily on your lovely photo, but they are so cold and hard and unresponsive through the glass—not like the real Bun's lips" (January 25, 1922). There are "blissful" dances in Oxford in May, leaving "as the only relic of our beautiful weekend, your evening clothes, your pumps (and I kissed them all again and again before sending them back to you)." She practises Brahms and Beethoven on her violin (August 14, 1923) and wishes he were there "so that my fiddle could tell you far more eloquently than I can personally all that is in my heart for you."

And he dreams, on March 3, 1924, of kissing every part of her "until you are glowing all over with one mass of kisses. Even then that will only be a tiniest part of the unbounded passionate love that I have cooped up for you and that is crying to get out."

And she, on November 21, 1923, has a dream "that you murdered me in the most blood-curdling manner, and I awoke very late with the Chapel gong . . . to find I was still alive."

It must have been almost unbearable. So they let their fantasies roam over what bliss their married lives would eventually be. His imaginings tended to dwell on long evenings by the fireplace, long walks in the country, and endless nights together. Hers often had a more social component. Win (April 20, 1921): "won't it be topping when we go and visit some of our children at school & college . . . I shall literally burst with pride when I go to Uppingham to watch my husband play for the Old Boys against our son."

They will have their honeymoon on the Norfolk Broads, in a sailing boat called *The Nigger*, which will be "easy to manage" (Bernard, April 14, 1923). They will walk across the Yorkshire Moors. He will take her to Egypt and see the pyramids. They will have their first night somewhere in the English countryside. Or perhaps the first blissful night will be in Paris, Switzerland, no, Italy . . .

On February 29, 1924, Bernard formally proposes: "Win will you make me the happiest being on earth and marry me soon." He passes his medical exams in May. A comfortable Victorian house in Hampstead is secured. And the marriage date is set at last for 2:30 p.m., January 1, 1925.

Win spends her last holidays with her family on the Continent in the autumn of 1923, and again in late 1924. The world is at peace and, for those who could afford it, full of gaiety. A faint whiff of the Roaring Twenties comes through Win's letters. Since the rich were often English, they felt privileged, enjoying the beauty of foreign countries while remaining supremely confident in the innate superiority of their own.

The first trip is to the French Riviera. This was the era of grand hotels, where the guests would dance in the evenings to live orchestras. There was an edge of dangerous excitement about the Continent, especially to a prim young Englishwoman longing for marriage. Win has occasion to observe about French and Italian men "that they all (old and young) stare and leer rudely and unfeignedly, they have cheeky eyes and they all spit copiously and casually without any apparent preparation."

In September 1924, Win, her mother, her sister Meg, and Walter are staying at the Grand Hotel Bellevue, a huge nineteenth-century pile on the shores of Lago Maggiore. Their "acquaintances" at the hotel include an English bishop who "has taken a tremendous fancy to Walter," as well as some "Austrian

*On the beach: Win (FAR RIGHT) and
Bernard (THIRD FROM RIGHT)*

and Parisian Jews." People on the whole are "very sticky" though, so "we have not danced with anyone except Walter."

The entertainments at the Grand Hotel Bellevue include a conjurer who manages to hypnotize his accomplice, "a pretty girl of 18." He sent her to sleep and "made her do the most incredible things." Her eyeballs turned upward, concentrating on the brain. "It seems to me a most dangerous thing for a man to be able to have a young girl like that completely in his power . . . He looked an awful beast and they were both quite exhausted afterwards."

One night in Venice is spent at the Excelsior Palace on the Lido, which is "impossible." All you get for the vast expense is "overdone grandeur and American millionaires . . . Everyone here, male and female, lives all day long in gorgeous brocaded pyjamas, with painted legs and arms, and jewelled anklets, and they play tennis like that."

In search of more "homely comforts," the Regensburg/Raeburn family swiftly decamps to a cheaper establishment, "an awful hole" actually, writes Win, because nothing else is available in Venice, "but I suppose endurable for a week. I can't say I enjoy 2d class living—this is my first experience of it & there is something sordid and shabby about it which rather repels me."

She cannot wait to get back to Bernard and England. Bernard promised her this would be the last lap before they can leave Oxford and Cambridge behind them: "You'll be mine and I'll be yours & we shall then be able to tear up all our note paper . . . our correspondence will then forever be one of the hand, one of the eye & one of the lips."

He wrote this on October 16, 1921. But the sentiments were unchanged on the last day of their engagement in 1924.

Four

SAFE HAVEN

———.———

According to family legend, Bernard spent the long-awaited honeymoon night writing thank-you letters to the wedding guests. The story, frequently retold, came from Win, as a joke at his expense. But I think she meant to praise him too as a paragon of good manners that we would do well to emulate. Bernard and Win took thank-you letters very seriously. People who failed them in this respect were not easily forgiven.

There may have been some truth to the story about the letter-writing honeymoon. In fact, I have seen some of the letters Bernard wrote to his parents on the day after the wedding, describing a very stormy crossing from Folkestone to Boulogne, and his securing a cabin for Win while spending the night on deck, himself getting drenched in a howling North Sea gale. That the story was not the whole truth can be deduced from several letters written many years later, when Bernard was in India. Being cut off from the family for three years, from 1942

Wedding in London

till the summer of 1945, was hard to bear, harder perhaps even than the long years of their engagement, but different in that longing was filled with nostalgia. Instead of dreams of future bliss, he fell back on his memories.

The Channel storm braved, they spent their first nights in Paris, at the Hotel Wagram on the Rue de Rivoli, opposite the

Tuileries gardens, almost half a century after Oscar Wilde had spent *his* honeymoon at the same hotel with his wife, Constance Lloyd. The Hotel Wagram is an apartment building now, but I found the letters H.W. laid out in a pretty yellow and light brown mosaic on the pavement. A plaque over the door says that Tolstoy once lived in the same building. Next door is a cheap souvenir shop selling postcards and miniature models of the Eiffel Tower.

In a letter sent from a troopship on the way to Bombay in May 1942, Bernard wonders whether they would ever see their old hotel in Paris again, which must now be "filled with pot-bellied cropped Bosch officers." A year later, writing from a dusty barrack room in Agra, he returns once more to "that little suite of ours at the Wagram . . . I can see it now, our little haven from the noise & tumult of a foreign city . . . Here I learned more of my love and of a vision only first revealed to those who have travelled far in patience and adoration."

During the war, the Boche had indeed taken over Bernard and Win's little haven. The Wagram was one of several fine hotels used by the Gestapo for their grisly enterprise.

They travelled by car through France, where Win was photographed in a cloche hat, her face turned slightly away, a cigarette dangling from her mouth, looking like a 1920s flapper. Thence to Italy as far as Naples, where they visited the ruins of Pompeii. Their private joke, recalled in several lonely wartime letters, was that they had to learn the moves of love from the erotic frescoes left by the ancient Romans. "And to think," Bernard remembers in February 1943, "that we had to get inspira-

Honeymoon in Pompeii   *Honeymoon in France*

tion of ways and means from Pompeii. I am afraid you married
rather a greenhorn but we learned a bit together as the years
went by."

Almost exactly one year later, Win gave birth to their first
son, John Richard Schlesinger. A year after that my mother,
Wendy, was born. The twins, Roger and Hilary, followed in
1929, and Susan was the last, in 1933.

Bernard and Win had got what they always yearned for: a
family. Devotion to "the family" was perhaps the most Jewish
thing about them. The family offered safety, protection, a refuge. It is a recurring theme in Bernard's letters, and intimately
linked to his idea of a "haven," beginning with the Hotel Wagram. Despite his penchant for rugged sports, army life, riding
motorcycles, swimming in icy midwinter seas, sleeping in the
rough, and other hearty pursuits, he cultivated a rather Victo-

rian idea of domestic tranquility, a mixture of English cosiness and German *Gemütlichkeit*, something Jews of a different class would have called *heimisch*.

He wrote, on August 9, 1921, "Oh, Win let me marry you soon—ever so soon and we'll get a topping little house with lovely flowers in the garden . . . a splendid little up-to-date kitchen where you can give masses of orders to our general,* a sitting room furnished just right, where you can give masses more to the same girl & pretend you have a staff of six . . . I mustn't forget the spare bedroom containing—why of course all our real art treasures and so on up to the chimney pots which show a tell-tale cosy fire downstairs and before which a very loving couple together in one arm chair etc."

The image of Darby and Joan, the paragons of connubial contentment in old age, celebrated in poetry and prose since the eighteenth century, often crops up in Bernard's letters. Darby and Joan are first mentioned in a poem by Henry Wood-fall, published in 1735: "Old Darby, with Joan by his side / You've often regarded with wonder / He's dropsical, she is sore-eyed / Yet they're ever uneasy asunder."† Clubs for senior citizens in Britain often used to be called Darby and Joan Clubs.

Bernard was never in fact the home bird of his fantasies. He was much too gregarious to be stuck at home for long, and home was a place for entertaining friends as much as for family life. Win, less sentimental as always, would not have wanted a

---

*A term for the household maid.
†Dropsy is the old name for edema, when too much fluid makes the limbs swell.

Sailing on the Norfolk Broads

In Switzerland

Darby by her side anyway. She too revealed herself in letters written during the war. Here she is on January 1, 1944, the day of their wedding anniversary, she in England, he in India, to "Bun, my beloved husband—This time 19 years ago I could not yet call you by that precious title, but it was only a matter of hours until I could . . . I know that had I married some ordinary, conventional man, however good & kind, I should inevitably have grown bored & should probably never have been able to remain faithful to him. But you satisfy all my needs, with you there are always exciting new things to do and to explore."

Not quite Darby and Joan, then.

The longing for a safe haven implies a residual fear of an outside world that can always trip one up. It is impossible for me to think of Bernard as a fearful man. Physically he was quite the opposite, and he was socially at ease with almost everyone (the only time he recalled being stumped for conversation was years later when he dined with the queen, but even then he managed to save an awkward situation by talking about horses, of which he knew very little). Yet he hated being alone. A letter to Win on December 16, 1923: "Sweet one, I would never have made a good bachelor—I hate my own solitary company so." He needed the cocoon of the family, the company of his wife. For many Jews, Israel is the ultimate safe haven, even if only on a symbolic level. This was not true for Bernard and Win. They were not unsympathetic towards Israel, but they weren't Zionists. England was their safe haven, England and the family.

The children were born in the first house Bernard bought in Hampstead, on Hollycroft Avenue, twenty minutes' walk from the house where he grew up, a detached Victorian red-brick with a white-columned portico, comfortable but not huge. The family moved in 1933 to a far grander Edwardian house on Templewood Avenue, with a tennis court in the copious garden. It was in fact a bit grandiose, the kind of house that now might have a swimming pool in the basement. They held musical soirées there, and fancy-dress balls; on one re-corded occasion, New Year's Eve 1934, Win and Bernard were dressed as aristocrats at the court of Frederick the Great.

In 1939, Bernard secured a more modest place in the coun-try, a small house called Mount Pleasant in Kintbury, Berk-shire, where the family found a refuge during the war. It was to be the main family house until Bernard and Win moved to St. Mary Woodlands, not too far from there, around the time I was born in 1951. Templewood Avenue was kept during the war for relatives who had escaped from Germany, but the fam-ily never lived there again, and it was sold soon after the war.

I have a watercolour picture in my study of the garden at Mount Pleasant, painted by one of my Dutch aunts, who stayed there in 1950. It is a very English garden with roses creeping up a redbrick wall, and flowerbeds tended with infinite care by Win, a sturdy beech tree in the corner of the picture, the safest of all havens, lovingly described in many of their letters.

Bernard writes from Delhi, on November 11, 1942:

> What a blessing Mount Pleasant has been in so many
> ways. The one I have in mind at the moment is its antidotic
> effect on the children against the rather luxurious life of
> Templewood Avenue. To me those days are now only a

memory—but the children must still have their life there quite fresh in their minds. My happiest times with you were certainly at Hollycroft and at Kintbury. Hollycroft contained all our ever increasing love and hope and aspirations. I lived through many anxieties there when you were lying upstairs and the family were arriving in turn. There I also discovered more and more what a priceless person I had won with whom to share my life. Everything was fun and we were young. Templewood was the scene of so many frustrations and disappointments for ourselves and for the world in general & those who were trying valiantly to stop it slipping into an abyss. I did not give up Templewood with any great regret. Now Kintbury has very special attractions. For us it was a peaceful haven from a mad world . . . the continuous ideal, better spelt Idylle in this connection, of home and England to me.

The birth of a child can affect the emotions of husbands and wives in peculiar ways that are sometimes hard to deal with. A mother's attention often shifts from husband to child to a degree that some men find disconcerting; love is no longer undivided. There is no sign of this in the case of Bernard and Win. Explicitly in her case, and more implicitly in his, however devoted they both were to their children, their marriage was still the core of their private world.

On February 13, 1940, when fear of the future was acute, Win wrote to Bernard, "I love my mother & my brother & sister & my large flock of children, but none of them mean to me what you do, who after all these many years are still my dear,

devoted love." For Win, at any rate, the safest shelter was always their island of two.

John, who was unusually close to his mother, must have sensed this. In August 1933, one month after the Nazi Party had grabbed total power in Germany, Win was on holiday with the children on the coast of south Wales. Bernard was working in London. She is wondering, in a letter of August 14, how she will get through the next two and a half weeks without him. She writes, "I miss you, and feel an aching void round my heart now that you have gone, as though you were still my young lover, instead of being the father of my vast family."

Then she adds, "John thinks it foolish of me to miss you, as he could quite well be my husband for once!"

Win with John and
Wendy (ON THE RIGHT)

Even before the grandeur of Templewood Avenue, with the cooks, maids, chauffeur, musical evenings, fancy-dress balls, and games of tennis before dinner, for which Bernard and Win would always dress up formally after saying goodnight to the children cared for by Nanny in the nursery, they led a full Hampstead life. There were evenings "At Home" at Hollycroft Avenue with music starting promptly at 8:30. They took pride in entertaining the Smythes, the "Jumbo" Monteiths, or Sholto Mackenzie, later Baron Amulree, as well as relatives named Schwab, Rosenheim, or Stern. Win, writing home from a holiday in Hampshire on August 20, 1928: "I am so glad everyone likes coming to us. I think you and I together darling have really achieved our ideal of hospitality—a sort of easy-going informality—and people like it, together with the complete harmony which they can feel exists between us."

And yet those worries about the impression she made on other people kept nagging. On that same holiday in Hampshire, Bernard had come down from London for the weekend with a medical colleague named Steve. Win had been "in a terrible slough of despond" ever since they left: "I am afraid the whole weekend was a ghastly failure . . . I feel so useless and *de trop* & horribly unwanted. Steve obviously disapproved of me . . . He was very lukewarm in his thanks and I don't suppose will ever want to come again."

Those thank-you letters again. Bernard's reply, sent from the Public Schools Club, 61 Curzon Street, London W.1, is one of many reassurances written over the years: "Don't be a Billy & start imagining all sorts of impossible terrible things . . . I enjoyed the weekend thoroughly. I am sure Steve did too . . . How you can imagine for one minute that he disapproves of you is beyond me! Did you expect him to fling his arms round your neck?"

Win's social anxiety must have been sensed by me, as though by osmosis, at a very early age. On one occasion, which I shall never forget, this triggered an act that was almost like a spasm of Tourette's syndrome. I must have been about five, or perhaps even a year or two older. We had been invited for tea by an old lady in the village near St. Mary Woodlands, named Mrs. James, who looked a little like a kindly lioness. Her husband, Colonel James, the one who is said to have muttered, "Don't like the name, don't like the money," when Bernard and Win moved in, had only just died. Win had impressed on me several times to be on my best behaviour, and above all not to mention Colonel James's death, for that would make Mrs. James feel very, very sad.

The sumptuous high tea went without a hitch. Mrs. James had outdone herself. Vast amounts of cakes and biscuits were laid out on the table. I behaved like a perfectly brought-up little boy. Win must have been enormously relieved. Then it was time to leave. As we pulled away from her cottage, with Mrs. James smiling and waving at us from her front door, I stuck my head out of the car window and shouted at the top of my voice, "Colonel James is dead! Colonel James is dead!"

I have never seen anyone quite so mortified as Win at that moment. She was white with anger, but also with shame. An edifice of good manners and proper conduct, so carefully constructed by her to ward off any chance of social opprobrium, had been brutally punctured by my impulsive act of childish cruelty. I had probably hurt the feelings of poor Mrs. James, but I should think the hurt inflicted on Win's feelings was many times sharper. And possibly that had been the point. It was as if I knew by instinct how to touch her rawest nerves.

Anxiety was, as I wrote earlier, "the curse of the Regensburgs." It is always tempting to find genetic reasons for one's own foibles, and probably false. All I can say is that I recognize Win's social insecurity. Which is perhaps why, already as a very small boy, I felt that attack was the best form of self-defence. To reduce Win's fretfulness to the self-conscious process of cultural assimilation would be too simple. It is hard to know what Win felt about her German Jewish background at this stage of her life. I'm not sure she knew herself.

When John was only one and a half, in the summer of 1927, she took him, his nanny, and his baby sister to Worthing for a few days. The trip was evidently a success. Win was glad they went, except that John "shrieked with terror & nearly overthrew nanny at the sight of reclining and quite harmless pigs, but did not mind cows or dogs, and loved ducks and hens. He is a good Jew!!!"

Except that neither John nor any of his siblings ever came of age in a bar or a bat mitzvah. Perhaps this was because the war intervened. More likely it was because Win, for one, didn't see the point of it.

There was, on the other hand, the charming man who ran the hotel in Worthing, a Mr. Schneider, identified by Win as "one of us." This seems a peculiar slip, at odds with the way Win usually liked to identify herself, since Mr. Schneider was not only Jewish but a foreigner.

Still, the eternal question whether so-and-so was "forty-five" was always on her mind. I must have heard such talk many times when I was a child, but the meaning clearly escaped me, even when my best friend in the first class of primary school was Wim Boekdrukker, who wore a kippa and stayed at home on the Sabbath. It was not until I was about nine or ten that the penny finally dropped. In the evenings, after homework, I used to roam around our quiet residential neighbourhood in The Hague with a small gang of boys who lived in the same street. For some reason our gang never included two brothers named Bloch. Perhaps they were too old for us. Dark and burly, they were also a little intimidating. One day, the oldest boy in our

gang told me, not with any hostile intent, or none that I can
remember, that the Blochs were "Jew boys." When I relayed
this bit of information to my mother, she laughed and told me
I was a Jew boy too.

Not much is to be gleaned about the state of the world from
the sporadic letters in the late 1920s. Family holidays come
and go, on the English or Welsh coasts, or at Mr. Schneider's
hotel in Worthing; Bernard tries hard to get a permanent appointment at one of the London hospitals, and carries on with
a private practice, his income no doubt supplemented by his
father's considerable wealth. There are rounds of golf, horse
riding, concerts, rugby matches, and nights at the opera. Win
plays the violin in various amateur orchestras and quartets.
Nellie Melba in *La bohème* at Covent Garden reduces Bernard
to tears. Win struggles with the César Franck Quartet. They
both drive cars. The garden in London is flourishing. The dogs
are adorable. Medical conferences are regularly attended, in
Paris, Stockholm, Leyden, and Moscow (in 1934). It was, despite Bernard's professional difficulties, a full and exceedingly
comfortable life. There is no mention of the Wall Street Crash.
Nothing about the rise of Hitler.

As the children begin to show their personalities, hints of
what they would become as adults, when I knew them, are
glimpsed, or so it looks in retrospect. It is an odd sensation to
read about the childhood of my mother's generation, since only
one aunt is still alive. Time seems compressed, and their lives

fleeting, because in retrospect everything happens so fast. In August 1928, on holiday in Hampshire, Win writes about her eldest son:

> A short story of John! Apparently yesterday afternoon, while out walking, mother and nannie went into an old church to inspect it. John ran in after them and said "Oo" at sight of the spaciousness, and was so pleased with the echo he produced, that he repeated the experiment several times until someone said "shhh," whereupon he said in a hushed tone "shh, baby asleep." He also admired the "lubby pictures," apparently ghastly stained glass windows.

Early intimations of the film director he would one day become? In August 1937, they are unmistakable. Win to Bernard, from Cornwall: "Things are jogging along here much as usual. The rehearsals for John's play seem to be causing a certain amount of bad blood, because he will take it so seriously . . . what I have heard of the rehearsal from a distance seemed to be excessively noisy, and I believe I am to be requisitioned for future rehearsals (O! Misericordia) to try and keep order!! If only John would confine himself to the piano."

By this time the world was already edging closer to the abyss. The question is when the signs of disaster were first detected by a well-to-do upper-middle-class Jewish family with German roots. We know that many people of a similar background in Germany chose to ignore the signs until it was too late.

The year 1931 was not a spectacular one. Japanese troops

Family holiday in Switzerland

had incorporated Manchuria as a puppet state of the Japanese Empire. The old field marshal Paul von Hindenburg was still president of the German Republic, his stern Prussian face glaring with watery eyes from the blue 25-pfennig postage stamps. Hitler was hovering, but not yet in charge. Lord Robert Cecil, president of the League of Nations, declared that war was never so improbable.

Win and her mother visited Kassel and Berlin in April 1931. The only hint of any unpleasantness is an offhand remark in one of her letters about Uncle Adolf, the orthopaedic surgeon, who seems "desperately depressed and quiet." He "is very changed," but she doesn't explain why. The reason may have had more to do with ill health, due to his heart condition, than any external circumstances. In the event, he died in 1933, deeply humiliated that a German patriot like himself, awarded the Iron Cross for his military services in World War I, would suddenly find himself unwanted in the only society he knew.

Franz Rosenzweig had died in Frankfurt in 1929, leaving his mother, Tante Dele, in deep mourning. (Soon she would be consoled by a female companion, an aristocratic lady down on her luck named Fräulein von Kästner.) But on the whole, life was still untroubled in Kassel in 1931. There was no hint yet of what was to come only a few years later, at least not in Win's letters, and perhaps not in the lives of her relatives either.

"It seems a far cry to Hollycroft Avenue & all of you now," Win writes on April 8. "Cassel is so closely associated with my youth that I feel quite unmarried & unattached here." She worries about getting fat despite "my spot of daily exercise," because "the food is so good." Everyone is "charming as ever." There are "pukka" dinner parties. They "get up in full evening dress" for a performance of *Faust*, Parts I and II, which, she declares, was "very interesting and amazingly well produced and acted—though Part II was incomprehensible on the stage." There is an excursion to see a "dubious light comedy by Molnar." They watch a movie starring Grock, the famous clown, which has not yet come to London. In Berlin, the Sterns—"as nice as ever"—pick up Win and her mother at the railway station. Ernst Stern, an industrial chemist, married to Win's cousin Maria, drives them around "in his lovely big car." A "wonderful programme of theatres and concerts has been planned."

One year later, Hitler would run against Hindenburg in the presidential election. He lost, but still got 35 percent of the vote. Two years later, when Hitler was in full control, the Sterns escaped to London, where they would spend the entire war in the Schlesinger house on Templewood Avenue.

On the last day of 1931, Bernard is abroad for a medical conference, and Win writes a letter from Hollycroft Avenue, commiserating with his difficulties in securing a permanent hospital job. She is worried, in a typical fit of self-doubt, that the first seven years of their marriage might have been a disappointment to him: "I realize how lamentably short of your ideal I have fallen, and yet I do care so much and I have tried so hard to be a good wife. If you cease to believe in me, then there will be no one left." She ends this cry with the "hope that 1932 holds something good in store for you in spite of this wicked world."

Quite what she meant by "wicked" is impossible to tell. Was she thinking of the hospitals that refused to take Bernard, or was she just emitting a sigh about the wickedness of the world in general? She was an avid reader of the news—in *The Times*, and after the war the *Daily Telegraph*. Perhaps she was thinking of the Japanese war in China. Or possibly it was the rise of Hitler and the brownshirts, brawling in the German streets with Communists, Jews, or anybody else they didn't like. That Bernard and Win were far from oblivious is clear from their early membership of the International League Against Anti-Semitism, founded in France in 1927. Together in June 1939 they attended a congress of the league in Belgium, which they found a gloomy and anxious place.

The first mention of the troubles in Germany comes in August 1933. Win is with her children in Wales. They are joined by a fourteen-year-old German boy named Reinhard, who, Win writes, "is not keen on reading." She is afraid that he must be "frightfully bored."

Reinhard was in fact Uncle Adolf's son. I knew him very well as Ashley Raeburn, a distinguished director of Shell and vice chairman of Rolls-Royce. Ashley, to me as a little Anglophile in The Hague, was the consummate English gentleman, who bore a slight resemblance to the young Prince Philip. I stayed with Ashley and his Welsh wife, Nest, in Japan in the 1970s, when he moved around Tokyo in a Rolls-Royce as Shell's chief man in the Far East. We used to play games of croquet on his vast lawn. The keen pleasure he took in knocking away his opponent's croquet ball was the only hint of his steely will to succeed.

Reinhard, as he then still was, had come to live with Uncle Walter's family. Walter had persuaded Uncle Adolf that his children would no longer be safe in Germany, even though they had been baptized as Christians. Reinhard arrived in England with fresh memories of Jew baiting at school. Possibly on Walter's advice, or perhaps based on his own instinct for survival, the German Gymnasium student quickly remade himself into a proper Englishman. By the time I knew him, the transformation had long been complete. But it couldn't happen soon enough for Win.

Fresh air and lots of exercise were among the main purposes of family holidays at the seaside. This, by the way, was not a fetish peculiar to them. Uncle Adolf had been a keen Alpine mountain climber. Healthy fresh-air pursuits were cultivated by many German Jews, perhaps as another sign of distinction from the pinched lives of poorer Jews in the fetid shtetls and slums of central Europe. After a long climb up the rocks, Win reports to Bernard on August 18, 1933, that Rein-

John and Nanny

hard "is developing into rather a serious lad, under Walter's guidance no doubt, and he lacks the sporting instincts and the agility of an English lad of his age . . . He doesn't seem to be enjoying himself unduly."

The other adults in Wales were a German governess named Paulinchen and a nanny, who "is positively sadistic" towards John "and rants at him like a virago for every misdemeanour." (John would nurse a profound loathing of "bossy women" for the rest of his life.) There was also a guest from Germany, named Fritz Schneider. I have not been able to find out who he was. But Win writes that he was "charming." Reinhard, however, "says very rude and tactless things to Fritz, who is very firm with him, and sometimes deeply hurt . . . Last night, for example, R. said to F. at dinner 'Bavarians are only a second class people anyway.' This may have been by way of light banter, but it was greatly misplaced. He always hurls all the misfortunes of the Jews in Germany at Fritz's head, and there are occasionally some awkward moments."

Going through the correspondence of 1934, I was stopped by the following passage in a letter from Win, written at Templewood Avenue on August 28: "'A Journey Through England' makes dismal reading & one wonders what is going to happen to us all and our children." This was written three weeks after Hitler abolished the presidency and became the führer, but still a year before the Nuremberg racial laws deprived German Jews of their nationality and made life unbearable. The only book of that title I could find was a compilation of letters written in 1722 by an English gentleman to a foreign friend. I cannot imagine that this made for dismal reading. I have a suspicion that what she meant was *An English Journey* by J. B. Priestley, published in 1934 to great acclaim. It described the lamentable social conditions in working-class England and advocated socialism as the only solution.

One might have expected a more pronounced anti-German tone to creep into the letters by the mid-1930s, but there is no evidence of it yet. In March 1935, Win is in Dorchester, rehearsing for an amateur concert to be held there at the Corn Exchange. She suffers from her usual feelings of inadequacy. On March 3, she writes to Bernard, who is now busy in London juggling jobs at various hospitals, including Great Ormond Street and the Royal Northern, "I feel that I'm not really up to it, at least not without far more work . . . The oboist is rather a typical German pedant—no quarter given, and he is far from satisfied with my performance in the Bach, so that now I have such an inferiority complex about it that I can scarcely play it at all. He is as a matter of fact a very sound musician . . . [and] quite the lion of the neighbourhood, being made much of by all the musical spinsters in Dorset—and they appear to be legion."

Bernard is entertained for dinner at the German restaurant Schmidt, in Charlotte Street, an establishment that survived well into the 1970s. The food is "excellent." He longs to take Win there. In August 1933, he refers to one of their temporary maids as a *Dreckmädchen* (shitty little girl), not a flattering term, to be sure, but slightly unusual for an Englishman who affected to barely know a word of any foreign language.

In August 1937, six months before the German army marched into Austria and jeering mobs in Vienna forced Jews to get on their hands and knees to scrub the streets with toothbrushes, Bernard is planning a Continental holiday, taking in Vienna and Paris. But Vienna is dropped at the last minute, not because the Nazis were spoiling to take over, but because he needs more time to complete a lecture series, still hoping for a job at St. Thomas's Hospital.

Then comes the letter, already mentioned in the previous chapter, written on July 2, 1938, four months before *Kristallnacht*, when Nazi storm troopers ran amok in all the main cities of Germany, torching synagogues, beating up Jews in the streets, ransacking Jewish shops, quite literally throwing Jews out of their homes, and driving the men into concentration camps, from which some never re-emerged, and many of those who did were physical and mental wrecks reduced to numb silence. The letter is written from the Grand Hotel in Bristol. Bernard won't get the job at St. Thomas's. "It is the old, old story," he writes: "(45) The senior job is not for me at any price."

As a consequence of this encounter with the "old, old story," twelve lives would be saved from almost certain murder. Before others, mostly British Jews and Quakers, tried to help Jewish children escape from Germany on the so-called *Kindertransport*, Bernard and Win had already decided to do so. For most people, the shock of *Kristallnacht* was the spur to action. My grandparents were planning to take in twelve young refugees several months before the pogrom of November 9, 1938.

The surviving members of the twelve are now in their eighties and spread around the world, in Berkeley, California; Long Island; London; Wales; Jerusalem; and in a retirement home near Tel Aviv. I have visited most of them on several occasions, and met their children and grandchildren at regular reunions. There is usually a photograph of Bernard and Win displayed somewhere in their homes, and tears well up at the mention of their names.

For six months the children lived in a hostel in Highgate, north London, set up by Bernard and Win to house them until they were evacuated from the Blitz and sent to various schools around England in the summer of 1939. Lilly Zimet, now well into her nineties, is the widow of Erwin Zimet, a Liberal rabbi asked to take care of the refugee children's spiritual needs.

Hostel children with Rabbi Zimet in Highgate

Lilly now lives in Poughkeepsie, New York, where I visited her on a warm Sunday afternoon in 2014. She pulled a photograph of her late husband from a manila folder. Rabbi Zimet, looking very young, freshly arrived from a camp in Poland for deported German Jews, is sitting on the porch of the hostel, strumming a mandolin and singing a song with the twelve boys and girls. Lilly offered me tea and cake, and talked about her memories of Bernard and Win, the strangeness of England when she first got there, the way she was teased about her German accent. After a moment of stillness, as I contemplated some more photos from the manila folder of my grandparents at various birthdays and reunions of the "hostel children," she whispered, more to herself than to me, "They were angels."

Ilse Salomon, Ilse Jacobsohn, Kurt Selig, Walter Bluh, Steffi Birnbaum, Irene Birnbaum, Lore Feig, Wolfgang Kohorn, Peter Hecht, Marianne Mamlok, Michael Maybaum, Vera Baer. Almost all of them were born in Berlin. Their parents had tried to shield them as much as they could from the daily humiliations that pulled a noose around their lives, little by little, ever tighter, until Jews were left bereft and utterly defenceless: the exclusion from public swimming pools and schools, the boycott of Jewish businesses, the ban on Jews in government service, the race laws, the confiscation of passports, and then the murderous assault on Jews and their properties all over Germany in November 1938, the night of broken glass when the synagogues went up in flames.

Walter Bluh, twelve in 1939, and the eldest of the hostel children, remembers how his uncle was taken away to a concentration camp on *Kristallnacht* and returned a broken man. He remembers how his parents, old-fashioned German patriots, realized that they were trapped, but tried everything to save their son. (They were murdered in Auschwitz.) He can still remember the horror of an SA storm trooper ruffling his hair, which happened to be blond—the difference between a friendly pat and a severe beating could simply come down to that.

What made the cruel treatment of Jews, the taunts in the streets, the bans in public places, the hateful caricatures in school textbooks, and the horrifying violence of *Kristallnacht* so baffling to most of the children rescued by Bernard and Win is that they had little or no idea why they were being singled out for persecution. Their parents thought of themselves as normal Germans, and were proud to be so, just as Bernard and Win were proud to be British. For some, perhaps, this torment was their first experience of being different, of being defined in the hostile eyes of others.

Walter remembers arriving at Liverpool Street station on March 16, 1939, on a train filled with refugee children, scared and bewildered by the cacophony of voices, public announcements in a language he didn't understand, lost children on the platform with name tags around their necks, whimpering with fear of the unknown, and then being whisked away by Win, welcoming him to England in fluent German.

After the death of Win and Bernard, a box was found filled with documents about the twelve children, mostly letters written by Bernard to get permission for this or that from various officials, but also German documents with the meticulous answers to questionnaires written by parents begging to let their children get away with their lives. The bureaucracy of persecution was extensive, lashing already broken lives with another layer of humiliation. What strikes the reader now are the ghastly euphemisms: fathers are suffering from "ill health" due to "circumstances"; parents have run out of means to keep their children properly fed, because the breadwinner is "unable to carry out his professional activities." Testimonies are included from former schoolteachers, praising the children for their obedience and sweet tempers. A letter from Michael Maybaum is signed "Meikel," which sounded more English. Perhaps he thought this was a recommendation. (Parents often spent their last cash to dress the children "in the English style," which meant that some boys arrived in London looking a bit like Sherlock Holmes in little deerstalkers.)

There is a drawing in the box, done in coloured crayons, on the way to England, perhaps, by Marianne Mamlok. It shows a train pulling out of a station. The train is marked with the words "Berlin-London." Children peer through the window at two adults waving at them with white handkerchiefs.

The question is not so much why Bernard and Win decided to help the children escape, for this was typical of their sense of decency, and a sign of their outrage about what was happening in Germany. Less obvious is why they decided on this venture already before November 1938. One of the earliest letters in the box of documents about the hostel is a surveyor's report on the property in Highgate, dated October 17, 1938.

I searched for answers in the letters, and found only hints, some of them written years later, when Bernard was stationed in India.

On March 24, 1943, when the Nazi death camps in Poland were operating at their full capacity, Bernard wrote from his billet in Agra, "What a blessing we managed to rescue twelve youngsters anyway from those fiends. Failing to get into St. Thomas's had a share in that." He doesn't explain exactly why, because he obviously didn't have to, since Win must have known. Was it because his own problems had sharpened his awareness of the lethal dangers faced by Jews abroad? It may be. There is, however, another reference, also written in Agra, a year later on October 24, where he tells Win about some money he is putting in a bank "for our protégés." He will ask the bank to "call it the 'St. Thomas's account,' for it was failure to get there which gave us time in the first place."

In 1938, Britain had pretty much closed its borders to adults trying to escape from the Nazis, unless they had sponsors or were prominent figures like Sigmund Freud, who arrived in May of that year, but even in his case the home secretary, Sir Samuel Hoare, had to be persuaded to issue a special permit. The only way some adults still managed to squeeze into Britain was to get a job as a domestic worker. There is mention in Bernard's letters in early 1939 of a German woman staying at Templewood Avenue going back and forth to the Home Office "concerning a new emigration scheme for Jewish domestics." Bernard mentions her once more on February 2, 1939: "I had a chat with 'Glucose' last night & worked the conversation round the English customs & thence to dressing gowns in the morning. She took it all in very good part—it had been ignorance on her part—and this morning we duly breakfasted together fully clad."

Glucose was Frieda Glucksmann. She had come over from Berlin, where she had worked at a convalescent home for Jewish children. Bernard managed to get permission for her and three young German Jewish women to work at the hostel in Highgate, not far from where Hitler's nephew was living at the time. (But they surely didn't know that.) Glucksmann was to be the matron. Just how Bernard and Win thought of getting the children out of Germany when the British government was still barring refugees is unclear.

Correspondence with the Jewish Agency in Berlin about the logistics of rescuing children began in the first days of November 1938. Their contact person, Edith Kaufmann, thanks Bernard and Win for sending clothes and offering to take refugee children into their charge. Frau Kaufmann wonders whether they could find other benefactors in Britain who might "make it possible for us to send more children to your country." Apologizing for any "inefficiencies" on her side, she remarks— one week after *Kristallnacht*—that "at present we are a little preoccupied."

It is difficult since the Jewish genocide to use the word "selection" in a neutral manner. Men, women, and children were "selected" on the ramps of Auschwitz-Birkenau, to determine the order of their murder. But there is no other word to describe what Bernard and Win had to do. In a letter from Bernard to the borough council of Hornsey, he explains that "for some months my wife and I have been planning to take into this country, as our guests, a small number of German refugee children between the ages of six and fourteen, and to be responsible for their welfare and education. They are to be children specially chosen from the professional classes about whom we have either personal or reliable knowledge."

They selected, in other words, children from families much like their own. Some of the fathers of the children had been successful lawyers, until they were unable to work due to "circumstances." Walter Bluh's father had owned a factory, which was taken away from him by the state. Ilse Salomon's father was a former classmate of Walter Benjamin. Like Walter Bluh's father, Mr. Salomon too was killed in Auschwitz. There was one exception to the similar make-up of the families. When Michael Maybaum, the son of Ignaz Maybaum, an Orthodox rabbi, appeared on the list, Bernard expressed concern that the rabbi "may not like the way his son will be educated as we intend to conduct this hostel on 'Liberal' lines. No Kosher food, etc."

In the end, Michael was accepted. Selecting human beings to be saved is of course a wretched business. But Win and Bernard wished to treat the children as family. In effect, they became their foster parents, concerned with their fortunes for the rest of their lives. They wanted them to "fit in." By rescuing these twelve children, Win and Bernard made it heroically clear where they stood. With all their efforts to be conventionally British, here was an affirmation of solidarity when it mattered most. But their allegiance was to class as much as to ethnicity.

For the *Kindertransport* to succeed, the British government first had to be convinced. After the shocking jolt to British public opinion of *Kristallnacht*, a delegation of Jews and Quakers pleaded with Prime Minister Neville Chamberlain to let at least some children come. In late November the government decided to allow an unspecified number of children up to the age of seventeen to live in Britain, as long as they left their parents behind and would not be "a burden" on the state. Not only did they have to come as orphans, but all the money to take care of them had to come from private benefactors.

The BBC asked for volunteers to open their homes. Networks were set up in Germany and Austria, coordinated in London by an institution named Bloomsbury House. Since the Nazi government refused to clutter German ports with refugees, the children had to travel by train through Holland, from where, until the last minute, when the country was overrun by German troops, more than ten thousand children were shipped to Harwich, and thence to Liverpool Street station, where the *Kinder* were met by their foster parents, many of them people with immense goodwill, often Jewish, but not always. Some of the foster parents couldn't disguise their disappointment when their allotted refugees failed to come up to their expectations. Pale with fatigue and apprehension, the children may not always have looked as sweet as the photographs sent by their frantic parents had suggested. Some foster parents used the children as unpaid servants. Some tried to convert them into Christians. But many lives were saved.

The first child to be met at Liverpool Street station by Win was named Hans Levy. He was not one of the twelve hostel children, but a distant relative—Win's mother was his grandfather's cousin and a close friend. Bernard and Win agreed to let Hans come to England and live with the family. A small, timid nine-year-old boy from Leipzig, who spoke no English, and had never met either Bernard or Win, Hans was taken to Templewood Avenue, where he was scrutinized by Hilary and Susan, his new stepsisters, through the banisters of the sweeping staircase. Within a year or two he spoke better English than German.

I only know him as Richard "Dick" Levy, now a distinguished professor emeritus of biochemistry at Syracuse University. Hans, as he was known all through the war, lived with the family at Mount Pleasant in Kintbury, before boarding at a local grammar school. Unaware of any difference between Jews and other Germans, the other boys taunted him for being a filthy little Hun.

Some of the twelve hostel children had similar experiences.

Lore Feig recalls how the teacher of religion at her school in London would make a point of saying that "the Jews had killed our Lord." Lore was also accused of being a German spy, supposedly sending signals to Nazi airmen flying their bombers over Richmond Park, where she liked to go for walks.

With the arrival of the twelve children, the family became an extended one. Bernard took possession of the hostel in Highgate on Christmas Day 1938, and the children started living there three months later. The girls slept on the second floor, and the boys in a large room downstairs. The home was furnished and equipped with donations elicited through an ad in the *Jewish Chronicle*. Some of the boys joined the local Boy Scouts. Schools had to be found for all of them. A "Hostel Newspaper" was devised. Questions were put to the children in English for their edification, such as "Who are the Mohammedans?" or "How did nations come to be?" or "To what extent do Jews often make themselves unpopular?"

Ilse Salomon (ten years old) wrote a piece for the newspaper about being an only child. She was always given everything she wanted, she wrote, but it was hard facing life all alone. Friends were not the same as sisters. And now that she was far from home, she realized how much she missed her parents.

Marianne Mamlok (eleven years old) also wrote about leaving her parents behind: "I couldn't imagine what my future would be like, as I had never lived together with so many children. I like it very much here and we get along well. I already have a friend here. But I would like it even better, if my parents were here too."

Walter Bluh wrote, "When we Jews go to another country

these days, groups find each other within a short time and play music together."

Rabbi Zimet contributed a piece about the hardships he had suffered in the camp in Poland, the freezing weather, the terrible food, the dirt. It would seem a strange thing to write for a paper meant for traumatized young children who had just been wrenched away from their families. But he meant to encourage them, perhaps, by showing that things could be worse.

Early references to the hostel children in the letters of Bernard and Win are mostly practical: shopping lists, bureaucratic hurdles to be overcome, staff difficulties (often to do with "Glucose"), financial dealings with Bloomsbury House, schools to be chosen, and so on. Staying at the Haven Hotel in Bournemouth in February 1939, Win complains of migraine attacks, but "the complete rest from 'refugees,' broken English & telephone calls will work wonders in a week."

Bernard mentions taking the children to the swimming pool on a Saturday morning in June 1939. The day before, he attended the evening service at the St. John's Wood Liberal Jewish Synagogue with Maria and Ernst Stern, Win's relatives from Berlin, the ones with the lovely car, who now had to seek refuge in Templewood Avenue. Bernard mentions meeting "a rather nice Aryan German lady" at the service, who "travels to and from Germany with emigrants. She is one of the Pastor Niemöller* group and certainly against the régime. I found her rather pessimistic about the future."

---

*Martin Niemöller was a theologian who founded the Confessional Church in protest against the Nazification of Protestant churches in Germany.

Hotel Alpenruhe, Hohfluh

And so Bernard and Win found themselves on the edge of the European abyss. The old life still went on, of course. Bernard tells Win about a concert at the Queen's Hall by the great cellist Emanuel Feuermann, who moved to London in 1933 after being dismissed by the Nazis from his job at the Berlin Conservatory.

In June 1939, just months before the German invasion of Poland, Win and her mother are in Switzerland for a short holiday. The tiny Alpine village of Hohfluh, where the local farmers in the foothills of the Wetterhorn blew their antique horns and carved fine pastoral scenes out of wood, had been Bernard and Win's Arcadian haven outside England. Family holidays were spent there since 1934. Win had long since overcome her scepticism about the grandeur of Continental landscapes. Here she is, on the eve of World War II, at the Hotel Alpenruhe

(Alpine Rest), writing to Bernard: "How far from the cares & worries of the world we are here. At this moment I am sitting on the terrace just seeing my precious mountain simmering white through the clean blackness of the night, the only sound coming from the dance band in the dining room."

There was no mention yet of the greatest horror of all, the moment when even England would no longer be safe.

On August 31, 1939, the last night before war is declared on Germany, Win is at Mount Pleasant with her children, helped by Laura, the cook who had already served Win's parents, and Bailey, the gardener and handyman. "Old Bailey," Win writes, "is being very decent. He said I was not to worry—if anything happened 'down here,' he would be with us very quickly. 'After all I was a special constable in the last war,' he said!!"

But Win does worry, of course. For she is on her own once more. Bernard, although past the age of active service, had enlisted in July and received a commission as a lieutenant in the Supplementary Reserve on the recommendation of Colonel Gordon Clark, his battalion commander in the last war. On September 3, he was mobilized as a major to a casualty clearing station in Hampshire.

Win writes to "My own darling Bun":

> I wonder how you are tonight. So far away from me! I hope that you will be able to sleep peacefully on your little camp bed. I shall be thinking of you all the time with the most loving wishes & praying for your safety now that this ghastly business has really begun. My darling, how I miss your cheery, comforting presence.

Anyhow, I am holding the fort for you, & having all our children to care for and protect, makes me feel braver. They have all gone to bed with their gas masks beside them, poor darlings. Luckily our black curtains were just finished in time, so we have managed to comply with all regulations.

Five

THE BEGINNING

———·——

The so-called phoney war, the lull before the storm, lasted from September 1939 till May 1940. Bernard, posted in various casualty clearing stations in England waiting for the wounded to arrive, and Win, now having to cope alone with all family affairs, try to sound stoically optimistic to reassure one another and no doubt themselves that things will turn out all right.

It was one of the coldest winters on record. Win, on January 29, 1940, feels "like a lost and forlorn little girl in the cold confusion of Paddington Station," the place of so many sad farewells. Arriving in Kintbury, she is overwhelmed by the "majestic beauty" of the wintry landscape: "It was simply breath-taking, like some colossal modern décor staged for an exhibition—a world of glass . . . A gale was howling, trees were snapping, the great icy wires clanked rhythmically . . . All the time the snow was falling softly, softly . . . There is no tele-

Bernard and Win at Mount Pleasant, 1940

phone or telegraph or electric light or wireless anywhere in the district, we are utterly cut off in a closed community. The children can't go out because of the falling trees, but it is all very beautiful. Everyone you meet takes it with a smile and a joke, in the truly admirable British manner."

The words are oddly prophetic of times to come, or at least the times as they would be experienced (and remembered, partly as myth) by the British at war, more or less cut off, the children sheltered from the wreckage, taking pride in the British spirit.

What was most distressing to Bernard and Win in those early days of the war was having to part from one another. Bernard writes on March 14 that "it is very hard to go off into the blue with the knowledge that it may be months before we shall be together again. That is the principal reason why this adventure is not quite the carefree show the other one was twenty years ago."

The phrase "carefree show" is an odd way of describing the mass slaughter in Flanders. But it shows how much Bernard loathed having to leave Win, and the wording is typical of the stiff upper lip that was expected at the time: "Still it's a job that's got to be done & the sooner it's over the better. Now keep cheery, fit & don't worry too much—no frowns my darling. I shall be back soon & we will settle down to a peaceful life again."

One month later, Bernard was on a Royal Navy ship outside Narvik, up near the icy tip of Norway, where the British and Norwegians, with help from French and Polish troops, were trying to stop the Germans from occupying the country. His last letter, sent from London, dated April 10, begins, "Just a farewell line wishing you and the family all the very best. I felt very sad as your dear face vanished further and further into the distance yesterday & I shed an inward tear . . . Darling you have been such a splendid wife & the future is going to be very hard without you, my dear. Keep the flag flying & don't worry too much."

There are obviously no details of the battles at sea or land in Bernard's letters, for they would have been snipped out by the military censors. Often, all he could send from "H.M. ships" were Field Service Postcards printed with messages such as "I am quite well" or "Letter follows at first opportunity." These letters, which often took weeks to reach the other side, if they ever did, include accounts of skiing expeditions around the fjords, his reading of *Tristram Shandy* or *Punch* magazine, sent by Win, and of sleeping in tents beside the deep blue channels, making new friends such as a Scottish surgeon named Benedict (Ben) Wevill, taking lessons in Norwegian, entirely without success, and such plucky sentiments as this, on April 17: "I think the good old British Navy & the allies have got this whole war well in hand &, who knows, I may be back for the children's summer holidays with the wretched business finished."

In the first weeks of April, it is true, the Royal Navy did well enough, despite U-boat attacks, which were not yet as lethal as they would later become. Ten German destroyers were sunk, and so was the first U-boat in this war, bombed by a plane taking off from HMS *Warspite*.

Win heard about these feats in the local cinema in Newbury, after a show of Alfred Hitchcock's *Rebecca*. An announcement was made by a man "with a very white face," she writes on April 15, that "Narvik was in the hands of the Allies. The theatre rocked with applause."

Tougher were the land battles fought against crack German mountain brigades and improvised battalions of marines who had survived the clashes at sea. The British had little or no experience fighting in Arctic conditions, nor were they properly equipped. But they still managed to hold on until the end of May, when the situation in France became so dire that the Allies decided to withdraw from Narvik and abandon Norway to its fate. It was during this retreat that Bernard had a lucky escape when a British aircraft carrier, HMS *Glorious*, was sunk along with two British destroyers, with the loss of fifteen hundred men.

Again, none of this is mentioned in the letters. But even Bernard, with all his optimism, can't disguise a sense of disquiet. On May 30, he reports, "We all listen to the news in the evening & try to cheer ourselves up with any bright bits which seem to be in our favour. It's often difficult to find them & we comb through it repeatedly in order to add something to the credit side. I can imagine you in England attempting the same thing. We must never despair, darling. Keep a stout heart. I still feel it will all come right in the end, but I am naturally anxious about you and the children."

Win's mood, especially when weeks go by without hearing from Bernard, is more brittle. Without him there is no one she can talk to. Surrounded by family, she still feels utterly bereft. To "Bun, my own darling," from Mount Pleasant, January 31, 1940: "Now that I'm thrown in so much on myself I find myself going back to a practice of my childhood; I hold long imaginary conversations with this person and that & I am really inhabiting a world that isn't real at all." On February 2: "Forgive me for being so downhearted, it is selfish & cowardly of me. I'll try and be worthy of you." March 3: "I am afraid you rather despise me for being weak-kneed, but we are as we are made, and I honestly try hard to conquer my rather feeble self."

And yet it was Win who took care of their five children, Hans Levy, two grandmothers evacuated from London, and the twelve hostel children. Hans, and Susan, the youngest of the Schlesinger children, were living in Kintbury, even as the older children were sent off to boarding schools. After the hostel was evacuated at the end of 1939 to avoid possible German bomb attacks, Win made sure all the children were properly dressed, received pocket money, found suitable places to stay and schools to attend. Every birthday was remembered, and all their personal needs met. In their memories, Win was unfailingly cheerful, a motherly centre to their lives, someone they could always rely upon. And aside from all this, she also applied to work several days a week as a nurse for the Voluntary Aid Detachment. None of her worries appeared on the surface. My aunt Hilary, recalling that terrible time, insists that Win shielded her dependents from any sense of fear. They didn't notice a thing. On April 10, Win writes, "I am trying to keep up appearances, darling, and I won't let you down. Only inwardly I have gone dead."

And the music continued, as it did in families all over Europe, even, as we now know, on the threshold of death in the camps. Win played the first violin for the Newbury Orchestra, performing in schools, church halls, army camps, and other public venues. Music, she writes on April 12, "is the only thing in life that makes me forget everything, and so at the moment it is a great relief of mental strain."

The relief is temporary. She cannot bear the uncertainty about Bernard. On April 18:

> I do everything quite normally but quite mechanically. Inside I am quite dead except for the constant gnawing anxiety. It is like permanently waiting in the waiting room while someone you love is having an operation—only there is no one now to pop in and out and report progress. I wish that my life could have been more balanced—that I could ever have cared for the children

half as much as I care for you. But I have always been
entirely wrapped up in you; at your side I could face any
hardship, any privation, any sorrow, because I love you
with my whole being. Without you I am an empty husk,
without soul or spirit or joy.

When I first read this, I was slightly startled, but not because her words revealed anything I wasn't aware of; they are
an honest and touching manifestation of her love. But the letter
is alarming too, for it expresses so clearly the dependency that
goes with total devotion. And it brought back to mind those
feelings voiced by her eldest son, in 1933: "John thinks it foolish of me to miss you, as he could quite well be my husband for
once!"

I have no doubt that Win's most acute anxiety in April 1940
concerned Bernard's fate. But there was another fear, so far unspoken, in the letters, and above all to her children. When she
wrote in 1934 of her dread of what might happen to the family,
she might have meant socialism, as propagated in J. B. Priestley's book. Bolshevism certainly worried her, even after the war
with Nazi Germany had begun. When Hitler made a non-
aggression pact with the Soviet Union in August 1939, she
noted that "Russia and Germany seem so cock-a-hoop and so
closely united. Will Bolshevism be the next menace? Shall we
or our children have to fight next against the attempted domi-
nation of the world by the Bolshevists?"

But she knew perfectly well that there was a far greater imminent menace, too awful to dwell upon, and that was the fate
of the family in case of a successful German invasion. That she

didn't voice her fear openly for a long time probably had to do with her stoicism, that "British manner" she was so proud of. Speculating on a German victory would have smacked of defeatism. And she made it quite clear later on what she thought of that. Defeatism was for foreigners, or, as Win called them in her letters, "foreign bohunks."* And this included some of the adult refugees she herself had helped to save.

The Sterns, for example, now living in the house on Templewood Avenue. After receiving a letter from Maria Stern, Win observes, on July 1, 1940, "I am afraid they have allowed themselves to get very bitter. Ernst was never de-Germanised and Hans [Stern] not much better, and I think that they might really do some harm to the cause unwittingly, by their extremely defeatist attitude."

On July 19, she returns to the same theme: "Mother is somewhat depressed, having consorted with the b—— refugees,† who are nearly all bitter and defeatist. Maria and Hans particularly are forgetting anything good they ever had in this country and are full of bitter criticism, dragging up every discreditable rumour they can against the British . . . I wish the whole lot could be carted back to their beloved fatherland."

There were exceptions, of course. Reinhard Alsberg, her young cousin in Walter's charge, had changed his name in 1937 to Ashley Raeburn. His attitude, Win writes with intense approval, was quite different from that of the b—— refugees. So

---

*"Bohunk" was an American slang expression for uncivilized people. It is derived from the word "Bohemian," referring to immigrants from central Europe.
†She might have meant "bloody," but "blasted" was a term that came more readily to her.

imagine his shock, and hers too, when he was in danger of being arrested and sent to a camp for "enemy aliens." This happened to a large number of German Jews who had just managed to escape from Nazi persecution, only to be suspected of forming an alien fifth column in the country that offered them refuge. On July 1, Win writes, "[Ashley] said that until now he had quite forgotten that he was ever German and that he knows only one loyalty—to England—so naturally he is cut to the quick." In fact, he had a narrow escape. A friendly policeman told Walter to make sure Ashley was out of the house during the day. Later, he was able to join the Pioneer Corps, made up mostly of trusted Jewish refugees, and after that the British army.

This question of loyalty was of cardinal importance to Win. More than during the first war, when the anti-German mood in Britain was actually fiercer, she felt the need to prove her loyalty, to make it clear that she was not like those defeatist refugees, those foreign bohunks who refused to be de-Germanized. Or like her neighbours in Kintbury, the Padels ("Ma and Padel," as they were known), with whom she made up a quartet to play chamber music, or another neighbour named Mrs. Rowse, who were full of defeatism and, in Win's eyes, Communist sympathies. When Win hears that Bernard has been spared from the worst battles around Narvik, she is relieved, of course, but still writes to him on May 8:

> I do hope that our Norwegian campaign was not just
> an expensive gesture, with no real determination in it.
> Next to you I love England more than anything else in
> the world . . . I want you to come home soon so

desperately, but England's honour would be too high a
price to pay for my personal happiness. I wish they would
hurry up & organise all of us & utilise all of you, so that
we could see this thing through as quickly as possible &
prove to the world that England is still on top & will be
browbeaten & threatened by nobody.

There is a tone to these letters that was lacking in her correspondence during World War I, when she boasted of being a
"lead-swinger" trying to keep her patients at Beech House
from being sent back to the front. Patriotism and anxiety not to
be seen as a refugee might be part of this. More urgent, perhaps, was the entirely rational notion that Nazi Germany had
to be defeated, not just for the honour of England but for her
own as well as the family's survival.

There is no direct answer to Win's fighting words in Bernard's letters from Norway, but his sentiments were doubtless
the same. On May 23, Bernard writes, "Pretty drastic decrees
in England were given last night on the wireless—a sort of
martial law but in the hands of parliament, it seems. I wonder
how it will affect you & our belongings, but I believe it's the
right step & will bring home to everyone that there is a life &
death struggle going on."

Like Win, he was probably thinking of England. But by the
end of May, when the German Blitzkrieg had already con-
quered Poland, Holland, and Belgium, was storming through
France and poised to cross the Channel towards England, the
unspoken fear became stronger than the fear of appearing defeatist.

On May 22, Win writes:

> Bun, my dear love—To-day's letter must be a very
> serious one, although I hate to worry you, but I must ask
> your wise advice & rely as always upon your excellent
> judgment and foresight . . . I expect you do hear news
> from this side of the world & you know in what a very
> precarious position we all are. If the worst happened, &
> this country came under Nazi domination, which Heaven
> forefend, it would obviously be impossible for us as a
> Jewish family to go on living here. What am I to do with
> our children in such a fearful event? I know that this may
> seem unduly pessimistic, & it is I hope a remote, if not an
> impossible contingency, but you always look far ahead &
> prepare for eventualities . . . Can you suggest any plan of
> action & one in which you could participate? I could not
> face the possibility of having to transfer the children
> somewhere without being able to get in touch with you,
> so that you knew where we were & could join us there.

Bernard replies, "I have thought much over that one letter
you wrote wondering what to do in the worst event. For the
moment I should stay put. I still think we shall pull through in
the end, but more about this when I see you."

Win was naturally worried about what would happen to her
children. But what terrified her more than anything else was
the kind of fate suffered by the parents whose children she had
rescued from Berlin. They too were patriotic citizens of their
country. Some of the men had Iron Crosses from the first war

Left to right: Hilary, John, Win,
Susan, Wendy, and Roger

to prove it. And suddenly their beloved country, the nation of
Beethoven, Schiller, and Goethe, but also of Mendelssohn
(Felix and Moses) and Albert Einstein, had betrayed them.
The humiliation of having everything you held dear ripped
away from you, bit by bit, was more than Win could have borne.
Becoming a refugee, to her, was a destiny worse than death.

One man who understood this perfectly was Bernard's
closest friend, Basil William Sholto Mackenzie, who succeeded
his father in 1942 as the 2nd Baron Amulree. "Uncle Sholto," as
he was known to my mother's generation, was a quiet homosexual medical doctor with a stammer. I saw him last in the late
1970s, when he showed me around in the House of Lords
where he had been a Liberal peer and party whip for almost

twenty years. This most discreet of gentlemen, always impecca-
bly dressed and diffident in manner, had a long love affair in
the 1940s with the art collector Douglas Cooper, a man known
for his affected voice trilling in a variety of accents depending
on his mood, his loud suits, and his generally outrageous behaviour. But Basil, as most of his non-medical friends called
him, apparently enjoyed the flamboyance of his partner vicari-
ously, chuckling quietly at pranks he himself would never have
thought of getting up to. That Bernard and Win were perfectly
well aware of Cooper's presence in Sholto's life is clear from
several letters in which they cannot quite conceal a hint of rivalry. Bernard refers to Cooper several times as a bit of a
"pansy." On May 2, Win mentions inviting Sholto down for the
weekend at Mount Pleasant but complains that "the old skunk
has never let one squeak out of himself since you left, although
he is supposed to take such an interest in the family. I suppose
the famous Douglas must be somewhere in the offing."

In any case, Sholto pops up again in a more favourable light
in a letter written on May 26. It was the Day of National Prayer,
for which the king had rallied the nation. Win went straight
from Paddington station to the Liberal Jewish Synagogue in St.
John's Wood, where she was moved to hear Rabbi Mattock
fighting back his tears as he told a packed hall that Britain
would prevail, even if the odds looked overwhelming for the
time being. Win writes, "After the service I went straight to
Sholto's . . . After tea [he] walked me through the Park towards
Paddington, and I came home feeling better. The irises in the
Park are looking magnificent, and my dear old London is look-

ing far too beautiful and dignified to dare to think of its destruction. On one point Sholto reassured me. He said I might be dead, but I should never be a refugee, and for that I was truly thankful."

It was the kindest thing he could possibly have said to her, and just the reassurance Win needed. Having established that she would never be a refugee, she could now concentrate on the future of her children, while demonstrating again and again her unquestioning identification with England. The retreat from Dunkirk, for example, in the last days of May 1940, when more than three hundred thousand soldiers were evacuated under heavy German fire by an improvised flotilla of naval ships, civilian motor launches, sailing boats, and even rowboats, sent Win into renewed flights of patriotic sentiment. She appeared to have completely forgotten that her own parents were born in Germany.

May 31, 1940:

My darling—What a brilliant historic retreat our B.E.F. [British Expeditionary Force] have made from the very jaws of death. I keep thinking of the Charge of the Light Brigade. What terrific reverses we always have in every century, & what undaunted courage and tenacity is shown by our men in every generation. It makes you prouder and prouder to be British.

Bernard's prose around that time is a little more down-to-earth. He mentions a letter from Sholto, who had visited Doug-

las Cooper in Paris, declaring that the city looked unchanged
and the food was as good as ever. "I fear," writes Bernard on
May 25, "he would not find the same now with the grim struggle going on over there. We all feel we are rather a sideshow."
Typically, Bernard would no doubt rather have been in the
action with the BEF at Dunkirk. But he concludes, "I prefer
not to think on war but on you all summer, as you describe
yourself, casting the years off with your winter clothes. If only
I could have just one peep at you again."

Win, however, continues in her patriotic vein. On June 3:

> What an amazing feat that evacuation was, but how
> terrible for the unfortunate remnant who were left
> behind. I am sure they will die to the last man rather
> than surrender. The men who have come back simply
> can't describe the hell it is over there, & yet they are all
> keen to go back and finish Hitler off . . . I feel that the
> spirit of all our fighting men is really undefeatable, and
> whatever we have to go through first, we must eventually
> come out on top.

There was another source of worry, however, expressed in a
letter sent on May 26, about a fifth column in the environs of
Kintbury. A master of the local school had been interrogated
on suspicion of treasonous activities. He was released in the
end, and the old man was in a state of shock. But since Win
abhorred his leftist views, she had limited sympathy and con-
cluded that he "richly deserved a shaking up." Laura, who kept
up with all the village gossip, told Win that there was a whole

"hornet's nest" in the area, held under close observation. Luckily, the wife of the main local landowner, who was "very true blue British," knew that Win was beyond any suspicion. Win still wondered whether she should continue to send her youngest children to a school harbouring "political suspects."

I have no letter to show what Bernard made of all this. But I know that he seriously considered sending the children to Canada. There is a mention in Win's letter on June 25 of an official interview with the children in Reading, the largest town in the county. The reason for the interview is not stated. But the most probably Canadian official "asked them when they were sailing & under whose care—hoped they would enjoy Canada & come back with a rich Canadian accent. So the cat was out of the bag then."

Quite what happened after that is uncertain. Later letters show that there was some kind of meeting in Cambridge, where the issue was resolved. Here is Bernard, writing from India on June 22, 1943: "Darling, how often do I recall that fateful visit we paid to Cambridge, our indecision & your final advice to keep the family in England with us. That, sweetheart, was perhaps one of the greatest flashes of wisdom that you have brought into our joint affairs & they have been many."

This meeting must have taken place sometime in the summer of 1940, before the Battle of Britain had entered its final phase. For on September 23, Win writes, "Isn't the latest German atrocity appalling, & aren't you glad that we kept ours here, even admitting the dangers in this country."

Quite what kind of atrocity she was alluding to isn't certain either from Win's letters or Bernard's. That the Blitz on London began on September 7 cannot have been a reason to rejoice in keeping the family in England. My guess is that it concerned the sinking of a British convoy in the Atlantic: on September 18 a German U-boat sank a British steamer named *City of Benares*. Of the 191 passengers, 134 perished. Many of them were children being evacuated to Canada.

Sholto was not the only friend who played a vital role in both Bernard's and Win's lives. Ben Wevill, the surgeon whom Bernard had met in Norway, became a close friend and often played chamber music with Win. Then there was a doctor named Gifford. Bernard had a gift for friendship, especially with men who used to be called "confirmed bachelors." Bernard's army friend from World War I, Harry, once wrote to Win that if he had been a girl, he would surely have fallen in love with Bernard.

On February 23, 1943, Bernard comments on their particular friendships: "Gifford was with you when you wrote. Have you seen him since? When I return we must have a party early with our two faithful bachelor family friends. I don't think either of them will marry now."

That he doesn't mention Ben Wevill, along with Sholto and Gifford, is puzzling. But this may be because Ben was possibly closer at times to Win than to Bernard, a situation that had caused a rare friction between them. In another letter from India, reflecting on their bachelor friends, Bernard suggests that these presumably lonely men found in the Schlesinger household a kind of surrogate family to make up for a lack of their own.

Somewhat more smugly, in yet another letter from India, this one sent on October 27, 1942, he writes that the "final proof of a really successful married home is a faithful bachelor friend & we have two such people which is as it should be & proves that our marriage has been twice as successful as that of anybody else."

Well, all this may have been true. But there might have been something else that explains these friendships, as dear to Win as they were to Bernard. Although this is never spelled out, Ben Wevill was almost certainly gay. In his long wartime letters to Win, mostly from Edinburgh, where he lived with his mother, Ben writes about his love of flowers, ballet, music, and his young "protégé" named James, who goes on holidays with him when he is on leave from the army.

Ben, Sholto, and Gifford were all Scottish. Bernard made one other lifelong friend in the army, a married man this time, who was from Belfast. There appears to be a pattern here, which I recognize. Despite Bernard and Win's devoted Englishness, their closest friends were from the periphery, as it were. One might even say that they were fellow outsiders of a sort, or, to be more precise, people who, much like Bernard and Win, came to the inside from a distinct angle. Bernard often remarks in his wartime letters how well he usually gets on with "R.C.s," or Roman Catholics. My aunt Hilary, who converted to Catholicism as an adult, once told me that he felt a special affinity with her faith. More likely, he felt an affinity with R.C.s because, with the exception of some old aristocratic families, they were never quite in the English mainstream, and indeed themselves had been subject to negative discrimination.

In any case, Win could feel safe with Bernard's confirmed bachelor friends. They provided male companionship in Bernard's absence, without posing the slightest danger to their marriage.

Here is Win on meeting Gifford in London on April 29, 1940: "I rushed home to make myself look beautiful for Gifford . . . I found poor Gifford pacing up and down outside the club, which was our rendez-vous, because it was closed on Sunday, so he hopped into my taxi and we went to the Piccadilly. He gave me a slap-up dinner, & even offered me champagne, which I rejected in favour of an excellent claret, and we watched the queerest people dancing, including a real gigolo!"

That the innocence of these liaisons was not always obvious to Bernard is revealed in their correspondence about Ben. Win clearly adored him. On May 4, when Ben is still in Narvik with Bernard, Win sends her love to them both and tells Bernard that when she is "digging and delving" in the garden at Mount Pleasant, she often makes "castles in the air"; indeed she was just "thinking what fun it would be if one day Ben could come out to Hohfluh with us all."

On June 4, she mentions her fears for the future: "I have never let on to anyone but you and Ben how incapable I really feel of coping intelligently if any awful emergency should arise. It isn't so much that I am physically frightened, but I am afraid I should just feel helpless & not know what to do for the best & everyone depends on me."

I have little doubt that her feelings for Ben were entirely innocent. But wartime separations tested even the most resilient marriages. Romance could blossom swiftly in times of crippling uncertainty. Some of these affairs destroyed marriages, some lasted just one night. Win's friendship with Ben clearly put Bernard on edge. In the autumn of 1940, he was stationed at a field hospital in the Kentish countryside, feeling rather useless. When Win was invited to stay with Ben and his mother in Edinburgh, so they could practice the César Franck Violin Sonata, Bernard had deep misgivings. As was so often the case, when he felt deeply about something, his prose acquired a slightly pompous tone.

"I am still not enamoured of your proposed trip to Edinburgh," he writes on September 29. "Apart from stupid jealousies and fears which you say are quite unwarranted, I foresee snags." Ben might find the presence of a "comparatively strange female" an "embarrassment at such times when he wishes to disport himself elsewhere." Still, he continues, Win is "old enough to know what is best." He realizes that "wartime leads to quick friendships & 'comparatively strange female' is perhaps the wrong term; still you know what I mean."

Win replies on October 1 to "My own darling" that she loves him dearly: "It is not likely then that I, a reasonable woman of advancing years, would do anything in the world that could possibly come between us. On the other hand, Ben is a man of the most scrupulous honour and integrity, & I would trust him anywhere in the world with myself, my daughters, or anyone else . . . I know that he is at least as loyal a friend to you as he is to me, and he takes a genuine interest in the whole family. Apart from all that we are keen fellow musicians—we enjoy playing together and we play well together."

To which Bernard answers, three days later, that he simply wants her to be careful, or as he puts it, to *"prenez garde"*: "You were always a large hearted little lady & have always got on better with the opposite sex. It is perhaps a characteristic of your family to jump into male friendships more speedily than most people and possibly more intensely than do those you make friends with. Most bachelors have curious reactions to married women, & particularly attractive ones, who befriend them and I should be very sad if your feelings were ultimately hurt."

Win, on October 7:

> I am quite sure that "bachelor's reactions to married women" don't enter in at all . . . I certainly have always got on better with men than with women, as you say, although I don't know any other member of my family to whom this particularly applies! According to Winnie Stiles I have got a man's mind & a man's approach to music, so perhaps that accounts for it . . . As a matter of fact I think that a respectable solid friendship with a man is stimulating and helps to keep a happily married woman from lapsing into comfortable matronliness & domesticity, and thus most definitely benefits her husband.

In the end, still against Bernard's protestations, Win does go to Edinburgh, where she instantly suffers from stomach cramps, but is too polite to mention this to anyone. Ben is "angelic" to his mother, whom Win finds "very domineering." Win fears that she has been "very poor company for [Ben], as I have been tired and unwell all the time & I look at least 150." They try the César Franck Sonata with another lady friend of Ben's, a paediatrician named Peggy, who plays the piano beautifully, "but it was a hopeless fiasco & I was utterly dejected . . . Ben has not asked me to play again to-day, and I don't suppose he ever will again either."

The curse of the Regensburgs again.

Ben's mother very much hopes that Ben will marry his paediatrician lady friend Peggy and settle down. Win thinks "he will one day too." Whether she still thought so after Ben came down to Kintbury with his friend James, I don't know. James, who was a housepainter before the war, has "perfect manners," writes Win to Bernard on October 16, 1941: "He wrote me a very nice 'thank you' letter after he left. I should like you to meet him. I think you would like him."

The only male who meant almost as much to Win as her husband was her eldest son, John. But in those early years of the war, he was a source of constant worry, not least because she found some of his ideas too "pansy." This was in January 1940, when John was fourteen. Quite what these ideas were is not spelled out. But John's natural inclinations were certainly rising to the surface, even if the signals were not always picked up very clearly by Win. On April 21, she writes that John and Wendy, my mother, were to hold a fancy dress competition at Mount Pleasant: "John and Wendy informed me this morning that they are going as 'Glamour Girls' and they wanted to borrow some brassieres from me for the part."

*Kintbury Follies: John and Wendy
as the Glamour Girls*

A full report of the fancy dress competition follows on April 23: "I wish you could have seen John and Wendy as the Glamour Girls, J. resplendent in my satin knickers with an overskirt of fringed crepe paper, Laura's best bodice stuffed with kapok and a chaste bunch of dandelions pinned on the appropriate spot on either side, a crepe paper bolero, my silk stockings . . . and a chic little crepe paper hat, & the pink feather fan hailing from Worthing."

Wendy was "very much made up by John," and the two of them, in Win's opinion, "really looked most fetching, & I must say produced two admirable pairs of legs, which would have done credit to any wartime show."

That John was desperately unhappy at Uppingham, his father's old school, was perhaps not surprising. Utterly unsuited to its spartan milieu, he was so badly bullied by heartier boys that he ran away from school more than once. On August 2, Win mentions what a "hellish time" John is having with "little prospect of a better future." Changing schools was not an option, however, for these problems have "got to be faced." Was "forty-five" perhaps a factor? Win: "The only other Jew in the house is very unpopular and quite friendless too apparently, but in John's case I do not think it is primarily 'Jew'; I think that is a good excuse for venting personal dislike."

Both parents agreed that John's plight, though unfortunate, should not be treated with excessive indulgence, lest he become too much of a softie. I had often been led to believe, by my mother among others, that Bernard took a harsher line in this regard than Win. The letters do not really bear this out. Three days after telling Bernard about John's hellish time at school, she writes:

> I'm extremely worried about John, and really cannot wonder at his school career . . . He is the laziest, most selfish & feckless boy I have ever come across. He is not interested in the world's affairs & seems quite unaware that there is a war on . . . He sits in an armchair all day unless forcibly evicted & listens to rubbish on the wireless all day . . . I'm afraid I must sadly say that our eldest son is a washout . . . Apparently many of these qualities are the cause of his unpopularity at school. The boys had him on the mat one day and asked him what he was interested in, or was any good at & when

he quoted music and drawing, they said his music was rotten and his drawing average. A perfectly good assessment, I consider.

Alas, the one thing John was very good at and took deeply seriously didn't find much favour with his mother, not yet. On May 3, he has "a hell of a row" with Nanny, "over the eternal question of one of his perpetual shows, around which the entire life of the community has to centre in the holidays. Apparently Nanny was uncooperative, & John was thereupon insufferably rude to her."

On another occasion, in April 1941, by which time John had been given a film camera by his grandmother, Win writes that John "is engaged upon his favourite occupation of 'making-up' Wendy as an experiment in cinema photography, and the twins form an admiring audience. It is all proving rather distracting from letter-writing."

The other member of the Kintbury household who caused Win much anguish was Hans Levy. His mother, Lotte, had just managed to get out of Germany at the last possible moment and found work in Oxford. Hans still had raw memories of *Kristallnacht*, when his father, already suffering from cancer, was badly beaten. He died several weeks after Hans left for England. Being thrust into a new family with five boisterous children cannot have been easy. Having to pass muster as a proper English schoolboy in Win's eyes, while speaking German with his doting mother during the holidays, must have been confusing, to say the least.

So, on one sunny day in May, Hans made a dash for it on his bicycle, supposedly bound for Oxford. He didn't get farther than Kintbury station. Nanny threatened the child with "all sorts of dire punishments" and Win was inclined to send him back to his mother. She relented when he expressed his wish to stay with her at Mount Pleasant. In Win's view, the boy was simply trying to get attention—"pure limelight." He should understand that she never made a fuss over any of her own children, and he would be treated just the same.

Responding to this little crisis from Narvik on May 25, Bernard is more understanding. The child probably feels "a little cold-shouldered" by the Schlesinger children, who see one another only during the holidays. His "equilibrium" must have been upset. Still, he writes, "I think your action in the matter has been full of wisdom."

This was probably true. Win was a compassionate woman, whose judgements expressed in private could be a little severe, but she was nothing if not self-aware. In a letter written on July 26, 1941, she describes her own children being criticized, quite unfairly in Win's view, for their lack of manners by Win's sister-in-law, Walter's wife, Dora. She writes, "Now you will understand why I didn't want to send our five children to strangers in Canada. It is always other people's children who are dissected and found fault with, whereas natural parental love overcomes these troubles. I rather feel that about poor Hans."

The year before, on September 13, Win actually had rather nice things to say about poor Hans, who was "not a bad little kid really." He was "a jolly sight more obedient than our own brats." But in his case too, the "de-Germanization" was not going as swiftly as Win had wished: "Unfortunately his table manners have reverted to complete Boche, & he has forgotten some of his English."

By that stage, however, there were more serious things to worry about. The Blitz had started in earnest. On September 13, 1940, an incendiary bomb fell on 15 Fitzjohn's Avenue, Bernard's parental house in Hampstead. On the twenty-fourth, Fitzjohn's Avenue was hit once more. "I can't help feeling," Win writes, "that the Jerries have a hunch that it was once called Fitzjew's Ave. and that you once walked its whole length in one of your gayer moments singing 'Christians awake.'"

On September 27, Win describes her day trip to London. The last two nights, she reports, "seem to have been very sticky." She finds a familiar hotel on the outskirts "completely demolished, belching forth bedding & odd sticks of furniture. Outside the little house a poor old man with a blanket round his shoulders stood among the wreckage of his home, with ARP [Air Raid Precaution] workers buzzing round like mad clearing up the mess." Picking her way around broken-up streets and unexploded bombs, Win inspects Swiss Cottage,* which is more or less still standing.

Bradley's, the rather grand lady's clothing store, was still unscathed on Chepstow Place. When the sirens went off five minutes after Win has stepped inside, "nobody appeared to

---

*A part of Hampstead where many Jewish refugees lived. A certain bus conductor during the war is reputed to have called out to his passengers when they approached Swiss Cottage, "*Kleine Schweizer Haus, alle Deutscher raus!*"

pay any attention and my assistant explained to me that they had spotters on the roof who reported immediate danger over-head. Later I went to the millinery department, & in the mid-dle of my discussion about colour schemes etc. the assistant suddenly said quite gently and quietly 'I'm afraid we must stop now and go downstairs,' and then I heard whistles blowing all over the house." Below stairs, Win relates, "the best joke was when my assistant carried on our business . . . with the enemy immediately overhead—'I think modom that this colour would pick out the fleck in your tweed,' etc."

Buying herself some respectable clothes in the midst of the Blitz was one reason for Win to come to London, despite Ber-nard's admonitions to stay away. The other was to deliver Tante Lise, Ashley's mother, back to her digs in Hampstead. Win was fond of her "Aunt Liz," as she had now become.

Aunt Liz had been staying with the family in Kintbury. This caused one tiresome problem, however, quite unrelated to the bombings. In Win's words, "Aunt Liz is a dear, but her German accent is appalling . . . To-day we went in and out of Newbury in a crowded 'bus (27 people standing, including my-self, both ways) and although she had the tact to keep as quiet as possible, she had to speak occasionally."

But the embarrassment of a foreign accent on the Newbury bus, though evidently serious, was but a symptom of a much greater source of anxiety. It was by no means clear yet that Britain would pull through. Win's feelings are expressed in terms of music, but this stood for so much more. Listening on the radio to "Depuis le jour," an aria from Gustave Charpenti-er's opera *Louise*, she writes on October 2, "It made my heart ache more than ever, and took me back to that dream world before the war when you and I went to the opera together in London, & Paris, & Milan, & Rome, in Naples & Berlin & Moscow & Leningrad. Incredible, extraordinary dream, that that could really have been us. Do you think it could ever happen again?"

Six

THE END OF THE BEGINNING

—·—

When the Blitz finally hit Britain in September 1940, with German Dornier and Heinkel bombers assaulting London on fifty-seven consecutive nights, the family, as well as the hostel children, were dispersed all over the country. While my aunt Susan still remained at home at Mount Pleasant, my mother, Wendy, her younger sister Hilary, and one of the hostel children, Ilse Jacobsohn, were at Badminton School in Bristol. This private boarding school had been chosen by Bernard and Win because of its "progressive" policies under the formidable headmistress Beatrice May Baker, known to all as BMB.

A tall woman with a leathery face, silver hair tightly pulled back by a black velvet band, and fierce blue eyes, BMB was a Quaker, a strict vegetarian, and a socialist with a marked enthusiasm for the Soviet Union. Unusually for a British boarding school headmistress, BMB was an ardent internationalist; she is

Wendy in fancy dress

said to have dressed up as the League of Nations at a Christmas fancy dress party, though quite what that looked like is not related. My mother recalls marching through Bristol with other schoolgirls in uniform behind BMB under a banner that read "Workers of the World Unite." Some staff members of Badminton liked to call one another "Com," short for comrade. BMB was also a lesbian who lived happily with one of the house mistresses, named Miss Rendell, or LJR. Apart from LJR, her favourite companion was Major, a Belgian hound.

Some of the girls were frightened of BMB. "Brace up!" she would bark whenever she suspected slackness. Every school day began with an ice-cold bath at 7:15, shared with gusto by BMB herself. She liked to encourage something called "Greek dancing," which I imagine as a cross between classicist fantasy and free expression à la Isadora Duncan, all bare feet and loose white robes. My mother also played lacrosse, without being very good at it. And she often recalled the tapioca pudding, which inspired hateful memories in generations of British schoolchildren, but I ate with intense pleasure when she served it at home in The Hague.

As far as religious practices were concerned, BMB was a free spirit. Girls could worship in any way they liked, as long as they worshipped something. BMB's own sermons tended towards the eccentric, ranging from warnings against the wickedness of hot water bottles to the saintliness of Mahatma Gandhi, or Sir Richard Stafford Cripps, the socialist politician who once served as British ambassador to Moscow. The novelist Iris Murdoch, who left Badminton just as my mother arrived, wrote about attending chapel under BMB: "Jesus, as teacher, shared the stage in morning prayer with a large variety of other mentors, including Lenin."*

BMB's regime might sound peculiar for a private school that catered largely to girls from well-to-do families. But it appealed to Bernard and Win for reasons that were not strictly speaking socialist. As a champion of internationalism, BMB made a special effort to take in girls from the colonies, including the West Indies and India (Indira Gandhi was there at the

---

*I found these bits of information in Peter J. Conradi's fine biography of Iris Murdoch, entitled *Iris: The Life of Iris Murdoch* (New York: HarperCollins, 2001).

same time as Iris Murdoch), as well as Jewish girls, including a
number of refugees from Eastern Europe. Efforts were made
to expose the pupils at Badminton to important world events.
Veterans from the Spanish Civil War (on the Republican side,
of course) would be invited to give lectures at the school.

In the autumn of 1940, the Badminton girls were evacuated
from Bristol to a seaside hotel in a village called Lynton in
Devon. Bernard took a dim view of Wendy's going back to
Bristol twice a week with BMB to have cello lessons, since that
city was getting almost as severe a pounding as London. "I
hardly think," he wrote on October 14, "two concentrated
'Cello lessons are worth Wendy's possible safety." But Win

thought it was essential for Wendy to carry on with her music, Blitz or no Blitz. After all, she wrote, "we must equip our children for a future peace time and Wendy's 'cello will definitely be one of her assets."

Hilary's twin brother, Roger, was at a prep school called St. Edmund's in Hindhead, Surrey, run by a headmaster named Mr. Bully. The school building, a huge Victorian country house, had once been rented out to George Bernard Shaw. One of the unusual features of St. Edmund's was that it had a nine-hole golf course, an extraordinary luxury for small boys. Since Hindhead was located halfway between London and Portsmouth, German bombers would have made a nightly appearance. Win wrote that of all their children, Roger suffered most from the constant air raids and sirens.

John, in a remoter part of England, was safer from the bombs, but still felt persecuted by other boys. Many decades later, at his house in Sussex, he showed me photographs of his time at Uppingham. Freshly combed boys in school blazers lined up in neat rows behind the housemaster, with John looking rather morose. He pointed at a tall figure with wavy brown hair, and remembered him with affection as the "school slut." Memories of nights spent in bed together engaging in various experiments came flooding back. Sleeping with boys, he said, was the one aspect of public school life that made him feel included. None of this, of course, is in any of his letters home.

Bernard was stationed at a girls' boarding school called Benenden, in Kent, on a grand estate that once belonged to William the Conquerer's half brother. The girls had evacuated the rather bombastic mock-Jacobean Victorian building, after which it was turned into a military hospital. During the summer of 1940, before the Blitz had actually started, Bernard was frankly bored, feeling sidelined, useless, away from any meaningful action, especially since the hospital still had no patients. His duties, among other things, included buying coloured napkins in London for the officers' mess, and having meetings with the man in charge of the local Home Guard, a keen botanist who spent most of his time nursing specimens of Japanese cherry trees.

The hospital in Benenden, in the way Bernard describes it, still sounds like a boarding school: the petty jealousies and rivalries among the medical personnel, the tiresome commanding officer known as "the Beak," a word I first came across in boys' comic books in the 1950s about English boarding school life. "It's a simply gorgeous day," writes Bernard on July 28, "and as I sit here on this seat overlooking these stately grounds with no sound but the flies buzzing round, a woodpecker in the neighbouring tree & the distant crack of cricket balls, I can hardly imagine that we are all at war & that the world is still so mad, & that perforce we have to remain separated indefinitely."

Curiously, one of the first patients to be treated at Benenden was a German airman shot down in the Battle of Britain. Bernard's descriptions of the battle, which lasted until late September, read a little like reviews of a sporting event. A letter from September 9 mentions having "a front stall view" of several "thrilling" fights. I can picture him, sitting in a deck chair on the vast Benenden terrace, pipe clenched in his mouth, a stiff drink at hand, watching the Spitfires and Messerschmitts circling overhead leaving puffy white vapour trails in the perfect late-summer sky: "It was a good score yesterday, 9 for 17 and apparently 40 bombers among the Bosch losses!"

"Last night," he continues in this same letter of September 12, "I watched Underwood perform a very slick and life-saving pulmonary operation on a Bosch airman—which was more than he really deserved."

Win's reply on the sixteenth is equally robust: "I am so glad that you are all busy on your proper jobs at last—and that the casualties are mainly German. That is excellent news. What a brilliant day's work yesterday. I don't think this has been such a good month for Hitler after all."

The extraordinary thing—or perhaps it wasn't so extraordinary, really—is how life carried on while the fate of Britain was being decided in the skies. A week before the German airman's life was saved, there was a dance party for the Benenden staff, which, Bernard reports, "went off well despite the continuous drone of Jerry planes overhead and the flash of many searchlights. I was orderly officer and spent most of my time seeing that the blackout was efficient. Somehow I was not in the mood for dancing & so did not appear on the floor but retired to bed fairly early and listened to a performance of the Fauré Piano Quartet instead."

The German pilot, after reviving from his operation, told Bernard that he had been treated better than he would have been in any German hospital. Hitler, he now realized, had obviously been telling lies about Britain. Bernard was suitably impressed. A few letters later, on September 24, Bernard returns to the subject of German airmen, this time in a somewhat cryptic manner. "Many of the German airmen brought down," he writes, "are found to be carrying 'what nots'—you know purple sachet things. They must think they are coming here to find [England] well occupied by their own troops. On finding out his mistake one fellow gave it to one of the troops saying that he would have more use for it than himself."

I looked up "what not" in various dictionaries, finding out from one of them that "what not" was sometimes used as a slang expression for male genitals. This cannot be the case here. I consulted Jonathan Green, the world's greatest expert on English slang. Even he was nonplussed. The only plausible conclusion I can draw is that the airmen carried condoms, for which they would have found little use in the POW camps.

There is no mention of "what nots" in Win's reply on the thirtieth. Instead, she gives in to one of her periodic moments of despair, the kind of thing she took exception to when it came from the "foreign bohunks" living in their house in London. The problem was not so much the bombs, which had been falling around Kintbury too; she and her youngest, Susan, had to hide from the air raids in a tunnel. But she misses Bernard dreadfully and feels "wretchedly depressed." The war, she writes, "looks ever more endless & complicated & the odds are continually piling up against us, and I just can't see any future for us, or feel any conviction in settling down with you to real family life again. I am so frightened that the 7th C.C.S. [Bernard's unit] will be packed off to the East at any moment now, with things blowing up to a crisis over there. My darling, I want you so, & I just can't bear this endless, & ever more endless separation."

Like many people, but in her case perhaps more than most people, Win was desperately keen to be of some use: "I feel such a skunk doing no war work when everyone round here is doing their bit." In fact, in June she had retrieved her old VAD nurse's uniform from the mothballs and tried it on "in readiness" (she was pleased to note that it still fit her). She also volunteered to work as a nurse for the Red Cross earlier in 1940, but was turned down. She explains why in a letter on June 26: "Isn't it the limit about the Red Cross business. One never seems to live down one's parents' foreign extraction . . . I feel rather indignant about this whole thing, considering my father became a British subject 53 years ago."

The name, always the name. She asked Bernard whether Sholto (Amulree) might be able to write a letter to the proper authorities to sort out her difficulty.

Whether he did is not divulged. But in October, Win signed up for General Service, which could mean anything from picking up the wounded after an air raid to scrubbing floors. She ended up scrubbing floors in a hospital near Newbury hoping to fill in as a proper nurse. But even there, doing her patriotic duty, she could not escape from her self-consciousness. "It was rather embarrassing yesterday," she writes on October 6. While having lunch with a large number of nurses in the common room, Win was suddenly addressed in a loud voice by a Mrs. Robinson, who said, "Are you Jews, because I think I taught Susan Jewish Scripture—not that I know anything about Jewish Scripture but I read her Old Testament Bible stories."

Win was mortified: "I got terribly red and all eyes were turned on me in some surprise. Rather tactless I thought, but she evidently had no feelings about it."

Once again, it is easy to mock Win's response. Why feel

embarrassed? But then it is an experience I have never really had; I don't look Jewish, I don't have a Jewish name, and I grew up in a country and at a time when anti-Semitism was taboo, at least to express in public. Even mention of the word "Jew" was best avoided. I knew, of course, that prejudices existed; I just never encountered them. Until one day in the 1960s, when I took a summer job at a solicitors' firm in the City of London, where I ran errands for two smooth young men who were just down from Oxford or Cambridge. They seemed perfectly nice and had the manners of the kind of English gentlemen that Win would have approved of. The name of a client was mentioned. "A Jew, of course," said one of the young men, whereupon the other replied, "Yes, I don't suppose you've ever met a Jew you could trust." I was speechless, out of cowardice perhaps, but also out of shock. I had simply never heard anyone say such a thing before. Perhaps I had just been oblivious, or too well shielded, or simply naïve. Perhaps this casual anti-Semitism was the mark of a country that never bore the stain of Nazi occupation. Bigotry of this kind could still be expressed unselfconsciously, as it were.

It was a small thing, nothing more than a vulgar remark uttered in a perfect public school drawl. But it comes back to me every time I read about Win's social cringes. She had to put up with something I never did.

Desperate times sometimes make people turn to religion, or at least magical thinking of one kind or another. In July 1940, after a visit to Badminton School, where BMB invited Win to examine a piece of shrapnel from a German bomb that fell onto the playing field, Win sends Bernard a "medal blessed by Cardinal Hinsley," which she sincerely hopes "will do its stuff."

At the end of September 1940, Hitler decided for the time being to postpone his planned invasion. The Luftwaffe had been unable to conquer the skies over Britain, not least because of a disastrous change of tactics. Instead of attacking the airfields, which the RAF badly needed to continue the battle, the Germans decided to concentrate on bombing large cities in the hope of breaking British morale. It did the opposite. But in the beginning of 1941, things still looked exceedingly bleak for the British. The United States was keeping out of the war. De Gaulle and the Free French were a noble but marginal presence. General Rommel's panzers were pummeling British and Commonwealth troops in North Africa. Benghazi fell on April 4. By April 14, the Germans were closing in on the Egyptian border.

On April 7, 1941, Win begins on a familiar note. Bernard, she claims, quite unfairly, could "return with complete contentment to a bachelor existence," while she had to deal alone with a house full of people, coping with the gardener, who was often surly, with Laura, who was often overworked, Hans Levy, who was in the early stages of a difficult adolescence, and with her mother and mother-in-law, who spent the war years with her in Kintbury. She then turns to the grim news of Benghazi being lost to "the blasted Nazis," just as Narvik had been before. "I just can't see how we can come out of this on top, and yet I know that we must, and that all this horror is meant in some way to serve the Divine purpose."

This is a remarkable statement from a woman who professed not to have any religious belief. Nevertheless, she writes, "I feel a great longing lately for St. John's Wood, and I wish you were nearer, and that you were there to share it with me." St. John's Wood is the Liberal Jewish Synagogue, opposite Lord's cricket ground in London. ("Lord's," by the way, refers to Thomas Lord, a cricketer at the end of the eighteenth century, not the Lord above.)

Bernard replies on the ninth of April from his new billet in Ormskirk, Lancashire, that, contrary to what she might believe, he has no desire to return to bachelorhood at all. He doesn't mention St. John's Wood, but says that he "prays daily" for the resumption of their peaceful life together. One has to keep hoping, he writes, in his typical fashion: "So for the time being I find the only way is to make the best of things, to keep smiling, not to think too much of the dangers that surround us."

Win is hardly reassured. She writes back on the same day that she still views the future with "the gravest apprehensions." What do Bernard's colleagues in the army think? "Has anyone any concrete hopeful theories, or do we still just 'hope' and 'have faith'?"

On the sixteenth, she writes, "I cannot imagine what it would be like to be finally extricated from all this horror—it seems as if it must go on for ever—or worse befall—but surely some miracle must happen to save our beloved England?"

Gone is the strident jingoism of her earlier letters (it would soon come back in less despairing times). She speaks of having "to cling to every straw," of forcing herself to continue "believing in the future." St. John's Wood, one feels, is one of those straws, that and the hope for miracles. But her religion was of little use to her. She made this quite clear in October 1940, when she wrote on "the Jewish New Year's Eve" about going to a service with Bernard's mother "to pray for so many things which can only be achieved with the help of God." However, she worries: "I wish I could be more of a help to her, but I'm afraid she misses the true Jewish spirit in me and so probably feels particularly isolated."

If anyone felt isolated, it was Win herself, without Bernard to talk to, and without the consolation of any particular faith, including the one that was nominally her own, to fall back on.

Bernard never fell back on the Orthodox religion of his childhood, even in his bleakest moments. Instead, he found spiritual solace where he could find it, including the Church of England, albeit doubtfully. His answer to Win's letter about hoping for a miracle is partly a reply to her earlier letter about longing for the Liberal Jewish Synagogue. He writes on April 19, "Your desire for St. John's Wood in these trying times I can well understand. Generally on Sundays I attend Church parade, although the padres who take it are not very stimulating."

His religious feelings are more clearly spelled out in a letter written from Benenden on October 9, 1940. He speaks of the Day of Atonement service at St. John's Wood, attended with Win and his mother. It comforts him to observe the holiest day of the Jewish year. "Try as I do," he writes, "I cannot ever obtain the same spiritual satisfaction from my Church attendances & last Sunday when I went to the local Harvest service I stumbled into a sung Eucharist. This meant a Communion for those who felt so inclined & that was the whole service. I naturally, in company of many others, did not take it & in fact, I found the proceedings & prayers rather curious & difficult to comprehend."

Returning to the Yom Kippur service at St. John's Wood, Bernard writes in the same letter, "Our prayers are especially needed for all those of the Jewish faith whose lot in so many countries is unbearable and their number increases progressively with the evil cloud of Hitlerism."

He had initially written the words "those poor Jews" before crossing them out and replacing them with "those of the Jewish faith." I am not sure quite why. After all, it didn't matter to Hitler whether Jews stuck to their faith or not; a Jew was a Jew and that was enough reason for murder. But perhaps that was exactly the point. Maybe Bernard preferred not to think of himself in terms of race, even though in other instances he did use it. If Win's feelings were complicated by the lack of a religious or cultural tradition, besides the German Jewish attachment to classical music, Bernard's sense of allegiance was not entirely straightforward either.

In May 1941, Bernard was shifted once more to another military hospital, this time in Bangor, Northern Ireland, a sojourn that a few months later provoked the remark that "we English will never really understand [the Irish], North or South. What unreliable people they are in these parts anyway." He was sometimes given to make such remarks. I remember him complaining to me once about the increasing number of "dagos" serving one on the London train to Edinburgh. He changed his mind about the Irish.

One of Bernard's last letters from Ormskirk begins with a

nostalgic image steeped in his particular kind of romanticism, which in his case often turned to the music of Wagner. Listening to the strains of *The Flying Dutchman* on April 25, he wonders "when we shall ever again put on our evening dresses & white ties & sally forth to Covent Garden or its equivalent & have an evening of Grand Opera together." In "this mad world" their former life "seems to be receding further and further into the distance." Still, he says, "the old Dutchman pulled through with his Senta after all his enforced vicissitudes & ill fortune, and reached his goal. There is a homily for us."

The homily is a little odd, given that the Dutchman was cursed by Satan to roam the world as a ghost until he finds a woman who pledges herself to him until death. A woman named Senta does indeed appear to save his soul in the end, but only by plunging into the roiling sea. The implication of this ultimate sacrifice, in the true Wagnerian spirit, is that only death will bring redemption.

The night before Bernard's Wagnerian reverie, he had dinner with Douglas Cooper, the art collector, who had been given a new government job interrogating downed German pilots when they were found alive, or collecting documents from their corpses when they were not. It was a morbid task that he evidently loathed, but Bernard finds Cooper much improved by his "various adventures—and he is no longer so pansy. By Jove, he can take his liquor."

One night at the end of May, Bernard goes to the cinema ("the flicks") in Bangor with the Roman Catholic padre, named Chamberlain. They watch a newsreel of Italian soldiers surrendering to the British in Abyssinia. The Italians under the command of the Duke of Aosta march past a British guard of honour with white flags unfurled. "This," Bernard writes, "was the only front where the war was conducted in any way on honourable and gentlemanly terms." But then, as he notes with amusement, the duke was an Old Etonian, keen on fox hunting.

In the same letter—and this is really the point—Bernard comes back to his religious feelings. He observes how he gravitates in most of his army units towards the Catholic priests, "who in every case have been such human people." But in the following paragraph he mentions a visit out of the blue by the Jewish chaplain for Northern Ireland, who, "seeing my curious name on some list, sought me out. He was a curious bearded gentleman with a foreign accent who told me that he was experiencing great difficulties in seeking out his flock as so many would not acknowledge their true origin."

Not being one of those, Bernard later pays a return visit to the rabbi, mostly out of courtesy, it seems. He clearly preferred the company of the Catholic padre. But when the padre asks Bernard in August to "read the lesson," he declines, telling him "that it would hardly be right and proper for me to do so and informed him why."

Win replies that she is glad he has met so many "kindred spirits," suggesting that she has failed to do so herself. But this was not entirely true, as we shall see. Music was the closest thing for her to spirituality. She would sometimes perform in a church, as this fascinating passage in a letter written in the early and still very fearsome period of the war reveals. Here she is, on December 9, 1940:

This afternoon I played through the first 3 movements
of the Handel Sonata in the church with the organist—
there wasn't time for more because of the blackout . . .
I am more frightened than ever now that I have
discovered that I have to sit in the choir opposite the vicar
throughout the service, & stand right in the centre under
the Screen to play. My fiddle sounded grand in the empty
church tonight & I love playing with the organ, but the
organist kept slowing down sentimentally at the end of
phrases as though it were a hymn.

This passage, as well as Bernard's musings over *The Flying
Dutchman*, made me think about the strange love affair between
German Jews and Wagner's music. The love, despite Wagner's
admiration for Mendelssohn and his friendship with Hermann
Levi, who conducted the first performance of Wagner's *Parsifal*, was unrequited, of course. But Wagner's music gave Jews an
opportunity to feel a spiritual affinity with German culture,
even revelling in their being German, without pretending to be
Christian. Worshipping at the altar of Bayreuth was enough.

In the spring of 1941, Win found her perfect musical match.
She joined the Newbury String Players, a chamber orchestra of
accomplished amateur musicians founded by Gerald Finzi, the
British composer who was most famous for his cantata *Dies
Natalis*, written in 1939. This deeply spiritual work was set to
the words of Thomas Traherne, a seventeenth-century poet and
writer of religious texts. Finzi, a handsome man with thick dark
hair, was a collector of rare editions of English poetry and a
devoted grower of English apples. The English countryside in-

spired his music. He adored the poetry of William Wordsworth. Ralph Vaughan Williams was the best man at Finzi's
wedding to Joy Black, an artist who helped to found the Newbury String Players. Finzi was as English as could be, his music
steeped in the Anglican tradition. He was also the son of a German mother and Italian father, both of them Orthodox Jews.

Win describes the Finzis at length in a letter of May 20,
1941:

> Yesterday, I went to tea to the Finzis—such nice
> people. They have built themselves a beautiful house on
> the site of an old farmhouse. It is modern & artistic &
> very practical. One room, which they call the Book Room
> is entirely lined with books from floor to ceiling; it has
> windows all round looking out over [the] heavenly
> Berkshire landscape from every angle . . . Finzi has his
> own study, containing yet another piano and hundreds
> more books, immediately over the Book Room . . . Mrs
> Finzi, besides being very decorative and charming, is a
> very clever artist . . . Finzi's own special hobby is fruit, of
> which he has planted a great deal. We talked about many
> interesting things, education, music, books. I thoroughly
> enjoyed my visit. I should love you to meet them—they
> would be a couple after your own heart.

She might as well have been describing the Schlegels in
E. M. Forster's novel *Howards End*, the family of intellectuals
with a foreign name, contrasted by Forster with the Wilcoxes,
who are very English philistines. Finzi's family background is

not touched upon in Win's letter, nor the fact that the house she described so lovingly was also a refuge for many German and Czech Jews. I'm not sure why she doesn't mention any of this. But in the Finzis, I think, Win had found kindred spirits, not unlike her own relatives in Kassel, but without the ponderous attitudes she found so disconcertingly foreign. Finzi never converted, so far as I know. But he certainly broke with his parents' Orthodox faith. Win never had any belief to break away from. Music was their shared faith, music and England. Finzi was English in the same way Win was. There would have been nothing incongruous to either of them about composing a cantata celebrating the Nativity in the Christian tradition, or playing the violin in a village church to the accompaniment of an organ, or indeed having the tallest Christmas tree.

In the spring of 1941, when Win was going around town halls, churches, and army camps with the Newbury String Players to boost the morale of the home front, British cities were still being battered by German bombs: Coventry received another Blitz in April, after being almost wiped out in November 1940. The night of April 16 was especially devastating in London. Defying Bernard's anxious advice to stay away, Win arrived at Paddington station the following day:

> We descended from our train—only 5 minutes behind time—upon a carpet of crushed glass, and we spent the whole day wading about in broken glass. Selfridges has been badly gutted by oil bombs, & I am told that Maples

got it very badly . . . There is a big crater near Marble
Arch, another at Goodge Street, and the damage
everywhere is terrific. The Globe Theatre (*Dear Brutus*)*
is gutted. In spite of everything, London life proceeds
quite normally—no one referred to the Blitz—and I was
deeply impressed. The trains at Paddington were running
in and out dead on time, and there was no confusion . . .
We lunched sumptuously at the Cumberland, complete
with band, & we saw an excellent show—*Diversion
No. 2*.† Edith Evans was superb. One felt almost ashamed
to be pleasure-seeking in battle-scarred London, but I was
glad to be there, & my admiration was unbounded for all
those Londoners—shop girls—actresses—taxi drivers—
everyone—who paraded for duty as quietly and normally
as ever after such a hell of a night.

One bonus of the war was the proliferation of culture in
Britain and for the troops overseas. Free concerts, superb radio,
educational programmes, cheap editions of good books, films,
many of them deliberately patriotic but of surprising quality,
were taking high culture into places where it had barely been
glimpsed before. Win's efforts with the violin were part of a
much larger enterprise that continued under the first Labour
government after the war, to bring culture to the people. I am
exaggerating a little here, but Britain was slowly being turned
into a nation of Schlegels, at least for a while.

---

*A play by their favourite playwright, James Barrie.
†A popular variety show at the time.

And yet Win's own children were often a disappointment to her. Only Hilary and Wendy even came close to her high musical expectations. That John had pretty much given up on the piano in favour of practising conjuring tricks distressed her. It shouldn't have. One of my earliest childhood memories of St. Mary Woodlands, only about twenty minutes away from Kintbury by car, is of John smiling at my childish wonder as he pulled coloured handkerchiefs out of a black hat. Although never more than an average actor (but a superb storyteller), he loved to entertain and insisted on others entertaining him in turn, which could be a burden for a young nephew eager to impress. John lived for the theatre. He was mesmerized as a child by the cinema organ that would rise in lurid lights before the movie began and then go full blast. The moment the theatre goes dark and the curtain goes up never lost its magic for him.

Bernard and Win were aware of John's artistic talents early on. How could they not be? For putting on shows with the family and friends, spending hours applying stage make-up to his sisters, turning Mount Pleasant into a rehearsal space and film studio, painting sets and lighting stages—these were the things he was good at and that made him happy. That is why he sometimes flew into rages when others refused to take his productions as seriously as he did; they were blocking his vision. This worried his parents. They wanted him to be more like other boys. There was no future in John's "hobbies." His lack of interest in anything but his artistic "obsession" was seen for a while as a character defect.

Bernard on January 19, 1941: "It is difficult to know how to help [John] become less egocentric, but it is all bound up with his inability to shine at things normal boys of his age can manage. Add to this a sort of spinelessness & inertia and you have most of his troubles laid bare."

Win on January 21: "I agree with you in your assessment of John; it is his spinelessness & lack of interest in anything intelligent or serious that worries me most." On July 19: "I think John needs to be encouraged to do something serious for England at his age, even if it entails a sacrifice—the better worth doing."

What she meant was some wholesome outdoor work for a local farmer, helping to bring in the harvest, or some such thing. Instead, John was entirely preoccupied with the "Kintbury Follies," a variety show that he planned to put on at the Village

Hall in Inkpen, near Kintbury. Win on May 28: "Next holidays are going to be a nightmare. [John] ought really to have been Walter's son, & then they could have enthused over their amateur theatricals together, but it is not much in my line, & nobody will be allowed to think and breathe anything else, & there won't be a corner of the house that is tenable!"

This is extraordinary to read now. I grew up on stories from my mother about the Kintbury Follies as a kind of legendary beginning of John's career. Everyone took part in these productions in one way or another, even the grandmothers, and so did Win and Laura. Once success came to him, no one was a more devoted supporter than Win. And in fact, despite Win's complaints and Bernard's worries about John's spinelessness, they were quite quick to reconcile themselves to his artistic aspirations. Such ambitions often end in failure, of course. They couldn't have dreamed that John would one day become a famous film director, especially at a time when the outcome of the war, and with it their fate as a family, was still deeply uncertain.

That John was unfit for the conventional life of a British boarding school was clear. They just didn't know what to do about it. It must have been terribly disappointing to them that he couldn't follow in his father's footsteps, be a keen sportsman, and show the schoolboy spirit that expressed their ideal of Englishness. This was particularly distressing to Win, who saw Bernard as the epitome of that ideal. But, alas, John was more like her, a dreamer, quite lacking in self-confidence, except in the life of his imagination, which he could shape and control, on stage or on film.

Bernard was perhaps quicker to understand him than was

Win. Without quite realizing it, he put his finger on one aspect of John's troubles at school. He wrote on July 30, 1941, "I don't think he is exaggerating his situation at [Uppingham] but am not quite sure what the 'old trouble' is—antisemitic or what? . . . In some young people, such as Ben, who I believe suffered similarly at school, it leads to finding a sanctuary in music if there is the ability . . . If only this war were over one might reorganize John's career and further his artistic ambitions and talent."

I am almost sure he was not implying that John and Ben shared a sexual orientation. True awareness of that came much later. But for all his jovial, rugger-playing, public schoolboyish exterior, Bernard was remarkably acute in the assessment of his son's predicament.

I have in front of me what is perhaps the first newspaper review of John's career. It appeared in one of the local Berkshire papers. A show was held at the Village Hall at Inkpen in aid of Wings for Victory, a campaign to get citizens to invest in war bonds. The paper notes, "The second half of the programme took the form of a variety show arranged by Mr. John Schlesinger. Amongst those taking part were: Marjorie Carter, John and Roger Schlesinger . . . Susan Schlesinger, Jane Spickernell . . . and Wendy Schlesinger. The variety show was an excellent performance by all the artists taking part and Mr. John Schlesinger is to be congratulated for arranging such a fine show. Thanks are also due to him for the excellent scenery and stage lighting effects." John not only wrote, directed, and designed the show. He played both male and female parts as well.

In the same column, a mention is made of the splendid performance at the same Village Hall of the Newbury String Players under their conductor, Mr. Gerald Finzi, playing an old English symphony, followed by Suk's Meditation on a Chorale and a Vivaldi concerto.

Bernard on September 10: "I am so glad the show was a success . . . John must be bucked & so must you after all your cooperation & effort to help things run well. Let us hope that John's persistence displayed in his theatricals will take him to the right goal in life. He will have to choose his career very carefully."

Bernard and Win missed one another awfully, a sentiment they expressed in every letter they wrote. But as long as Bernard was posted somewhere in the British Isles, Win could at least visit him from time to time, taking trains, and even planes when he was in Northern Ireland, with her violin and a suitcase with her evening dresses. They could write letters in the expectation that they would arrive in a few days. They could even telephone. The news she dreaded most of all was something she had already anticipated in 1940; that he would be "packed off to the East," out of reach, God knows where and exposed to what dangers.

The order came in February 1942. He was as disturbed by it as she was, but expressed this with the forced cheerfulness and slightly clichéd prose that he usually adopted when he felt things most profoundly. His last letter in England was written on February 12 from a pub called the Red Lion in Hatfield, Hertfordshire:

I am sitting in one now deserted & rather shambly
room, with memories of your dear self still haunting it.
Oh the partings. A dark cloud passed over the sun as
your train steamed out this morning. I fear it may stay
below the horizon for some considerable time for that is
my rather gloomy vista whenever you are away from me.
Eventually, however, I feel convinced that the sun will
shine again, we shall all be reunited . . . and live happily
ever after like all the good story books.

Her letter, now addressed on the envelope to Lt. Colonel
B. E. Schlesinger, is sent two days later:

My dearest beloved—I wonder so much where you
are & how you are faring, & where you are bound for?
My thoughts are with you ceaselessly, while I try to
picture the unknown. It is very terrible to have a part of
oneself so cut off that you know not where they are, nor
whither they are bound . . . It is only a week ago today
since we laughed together chez Messrs Potash and
Perlmutter,* since we met N. at the Conservative Club,
lunched at Prunier's & dined at the Berkeley, & already it
seems like a dream; and one has returned to a world of
gnawing anxiety. I pray to God constantly for you, my
darling, & for our poor hard-pressed country.

Potash and Perlmutter was a Jewish film comedy made in Hollywood in 1923.
They both adored it, unlike the Marx Brothers films, which Bernard declares in
a letter sent on October 3, 1941, "a disservice to our fraternity."

Seven

EMPIRE

—·—

F or more than a month, straddling March and April 1942, Bernard was on board a ship transporting soldiers and nurses, many of whom, he later related to Win, ended up getting married to one another—it was a long trip. Neither Bernard nor Win had any idea where he was bound. The destination was a closely held military secret. Bernard's messages would arrive in Kintbury in envelopes stamped "Received from H.M. ships" and "passed by censors."

Letters would normally take at least a month to reach the other side, if they arrived at all, even once Bernard had landed at his final destination, a situation that would last until near the end of the war. This didn't prevent them from writing almost every day. Some were long letters sent by airmail, all of them carefully numbered, and some were "airgraphs," a technique developed by the Kodak company whereby short letters were photographed and sent on microfilm. These would normally go quicker. Everything had to pass through military censorship, which made Win nervous about Bernard's more amorous effusions.

Bernard's fairly cushy job en route was to look after the health of the officers on board. The rest of his time was spent reading and dining, as well as playing poker and deck tennis. That he passed along the coast of Africa seems clear from his descriptions of palm trees on the horizon and the sight of "a primitive bark canoe being skilfully paddled by a coal black native wearing only something around his middle as seems customary."

In the last week of March he is ashore in a "very pleasant port," where "people are most hospitable" and "all the clubs have thrown open their doors and made us honorary members during our fleeting visit." One of Bernard's habits in any new place was to find the nearest squash court. Several old friends from his time in Northern Ireland happened to be in the same port city, one of whom, after spending some time there, "looks almost as black as the natives who provide the labour and service everywhere." As though to make sure he is not misunderstood, Bernard has pencilled in the words "from the sun" after "black." Subsequent letters make it clear that the port city in question was Cape Town in South Africa.

Back on board, Bernard attends a Sunday-morning church service, preceded, he writes on April 4, by "the usual short record of church bells broadcast throughout the ship—a pleasant English country sound which I fear will not be heard in reality until Armistice Day."

By then, Bernard had clearly received some letters from

Win, probably picked up in Cape Town, for there is a slightly mysterious reference in his letter of March 29, which goes, "We left the Sch problem rather in abeyance. If the family are still keen I think they should drop the ch each at a propitious moment."

A letter sent by Win on March 3 solves the mystery. While Bernard was being shipped off to God knows where, Win was facing two family problems, one a kind of moral panic about sexual misdeeds, to which I shall return presently, the other to do, yet again, with the family name. In his father's absence, John had decided that the name sounded too German. Schlesinger was no good for the stage. It would look odd on the cast list of his "theatre company." The "ch" at least should be dropped. Quite what stage name John had in mind is unknown: Slazenger, perhaps, like the sporting goods manufacturer, or Slesinger maybe? Apparently he couldn't make up his mind. Win, in any case, disapproves: "I don't want him to get ashamed of his father's name, and if he ever honours it as much as his father has done he will be lucky. I told John that if his existing name will wreck the 'company,' the company will just have to forego his services."

That Win, who was usually keener than Bernard to shed the marks of a foreign background, should stand up for the family name might seem unexpected, but her reasons were wholly in character. What mattered most to her was her husband's honour. Then again, she had not followed her brother Walter's example in World War I to change Regensburg to Raeburn either. Bernard was more flexible on this vexing aspect of Jewish assimilation.

The matter of the family name would be batted back and forth in various letters and not really resolved until well into the next year. On June 26, 1942, Bernard writes that "if the children don't want to be saddled with an Sch, and feel very strongly about it, steps should be taken . . . to alter it. But they should remember that more depends on what sort of people they are and how they behave than on what they are called."

The question is finally settled in the spring of 1943. Various people have expressed an opinion, including John's house-master at Uppingham, and faithful Sholto, who had by then inherited his father's title of Lord Amulree. "Re the name," Win writes on May 23, "we have practically decided to do nothing about it. You have made the name so worthy & well known both in the medical and the military world, that we think it wiser to keep your name. Sholto profoundly disagrees with changing it; he thinks that it shows lack of character."

The other problem, about sexual behaviour, was a little more dramatic. One might have expected their eldest son's fondness for dressing up in his mother's clothes, applying make-up to his sisters, and playing female parts in variety shows to have caused Bernard and Win some concern. The word "pansy" does indeed crop up in various letters describing John's conduct. But the moral panic in this instance did not involve him, but rather Hans Levy. He had already caused alarm by running away once, supposedly to join his mother, Lotte, in Oxford. And Win had disapproved of his "Boche" table manners. Now he appeared to have got himself into even worse trouble.

Hans was twelve in 1942. Win worries that he has what she calls, in a letter written on March 2, "a moral defect." He had

written to his mother about being "lovesick." An "unsavoury
episode" had supposedly taken place during the summer holiday between young Hans and an older girl of "unsavoury reputation." In a letter sent on the twenty-fourth, Bernard is
informed that their bachelor friends Gifford and Ben have
been consulted and they "take a very serious view of it." Indeed, they feel strongly that Win should not allow Hans to stay
in the house; he would have a corrupting influence on the children. They recommend a child psychiatrist named Dr. Mildred
Creak.

Dr. Creak was a little distracted by other things during her
session with Hans, but she did have time to ask whether he was
"involved in any homosexual business at school." A letter of
inquiry was sent forthwith to Mr. Harley, the headmaster of
Hans's grammar school. Mr. Harley was not helpful, had
"rather reactionary views," according to Win, was "fed up with
refugees" too, but agreed to send the boy for treatment to a
Child Guidance Clinic. The doctor at the clinic took one look
at him and said, "There is a typical potential pansy boy &
homosexual."

Mr. Harley then told Win—who was by that stage beside
herself with worry—that he no longer approved of the Child
Guidance Clinic. It was either that or his grammar school,
where he promised to take the boy in hand with "the paste on
the pants" method. Win, on reflection, chose to stick with the
school, and rather regretted that she had ever consulted Gifford and Ben on the Hans question.

Bernard only gets wind of the moral panic much later. On
June 28, by now posted at the British Military Hospital in

*Hans Levy (RIGHT) in a school
production of* The Mikado

Delhi, he declares himself "a little bewildered by all this Child Guidance Clinic treatment." On the thirtieth he writes entirely sensibly that "Hans's problems are those mainly of adolescence apparently and will no doubt pass."

Nothing more is heard of the affair after that. Indeed, little Hans would make a full recovery in Win's estimation. I called Professor "Dick" Levy at his house in Syracuse, New York, to ask him about this episode, wondering if I should even mention it at all, not wishing to cause any distress, even sixty years after the event. He told me he could not remember any of it.

On February 27, 1944, Win writes that Hans "has grown

into such a charming, sensible & quiet lad. He is certainly a case of a brand snatched from the burning,* when you think of the highly strung, noisy, exhibitionist little fellow who came over here 5 years ago. An English boarding school has worked the miracle."

It is all rather astonishing to read now. Win's trust in the English boarding school as the vehicle of salvation is perhaps a bit naïve, considering what went on at English boarding schools, but not at all surprising. And her panic was at least partly due to her having to deal with family crises on her own. Bernard's quiet wisdom is not unexpected either. What strikes the modern reader as extraordinary, though, is the conclusion drawn even by a prominent child psychiatrist, later well known for her work on autism, that any sign of sexual precociousness would have to be linked to homosexuality. After all, the whole affair was sparked by a story of impropriety with an older girl. That John, in spite of his "pansy" predilections, was above suspicion suggests that many adults had a rather hazy idea of homosexuality. Or maybe there were suspicions, but they were projected onto poor Hans. Or perhaps one form of "perversity" was assumed to be automatically the result of another.†

I don't know. But reading about this incident brought to mind a moral panic in my own youth. I was exactly the same age

---

*The proper citation from the Old Testament is, "I have overthrown some of you, as God overthrew Sodom and Gomorrah, and you were as a firebrand plucked from the burning" (Amos 4:11). Sinners who repent can still be saved by divine mercy.
†A further twist of irony is that John's headmaster at Uppingham was John Wolfenden, who as Lord Wolfenden published the famous Wolfenden Report in 1957, recommending that homosexual acts between consenting adults should be legal.

as Hans, at the time of his affair with the older girl, when my father was greatly concerned about my friendship with A., an amiable fellow two years older than myself. We used to go bicycling in the dunes a few miles from our house in The Hague. One day my father took me aside and quizzed me in a rather diffident manner about the nature of my friendship with A.

"What do you mean?" I said.

"Well," he replied, "what do you get up to in the dunes?"

"We go cycling," I said.

"Yes, but do you do anything else?

"Like what?"

"Play games."

"What games?"

"Like pulling each other's dicks."

I was flabbergasted by this suggestion. So flabbergasted that I put it to A. that we would surely never do any such thing. A. was not too bright, but he knew enough to be deeply offended. I never saw much of him after that.

Perhaps it was in the way of a small and barely conscious act of vengeance that some years later, after having stayed with my uncle John in London, I delighted in irritating my father by mimicking John's mannerisms. Having been picked up from the ferryboat at Hook of Holland, I would regale my parents in the fruitiest voice I could muster about all the "sweet, sweet people" I had met in London, watching my poor father's shoulders tense up behind the steering wheel.

Something had changed in the delicate relations between children and parents since 1942, but perhaps not as much as one might have assumed.

As reticent as Bernard was about his experiences in the first war, he loved to tell us stories about India, not just about the relative merits of squash courts in 'Pindi or Agra, but the sounds, the sights, the different ways of dressing among Hindus and Muslims, and the pleasure of having a "punkha wallah" provide a cool breeze in the tropical heat by manually working a large fan. However, his nostalgia—"Best since India!" he would shout to amuse us, prompted by a particularly good lunch or the sweet smell of a fine cheroot—was for British India. I asked him once whether he ever wanted to go back. "Not really," he replied. "Too much has changed since my time."

Bernard's views on India and Indians, especially in the early stages of his stay there, were conventional for an Englishman of his class. On December 13, 1942, he writes from the British Military Hospital in Delhi, "The average Indian has a child's mentality. I find the best way to get on with them is to treat them with a mixture of strictness aggravated occasionally with a tempestuous outburst, with a degree of encouragement & whenever possible with a twinkle, as most of them have a child-like sense of humour."

Like most Europeans who held positions of paternalistic authority in the colonies, Bernard didn't quite realize that the "child's mentality," the offended sulks, the playing dumb, were the natural reflexes of colonized people everywhere, the small covert acts of resistance that mitigate the sense of humiliation.

The spicy curries served in the houses of Indian colleagues

Bernard in Delhi

late in the evening, after endless rounds of drinks, he found "interesting" but bad for his digestion. Indian music, he declares on June 19, "which brays forth in demi semi tones when I switch on the wireless just leaves me cold." And some of the Indian customs he finds quite baffling. On June 30, in the same letter where he talks about Hans and his adolescent problems, he describes treating the wife of his "bearer," a Muslim, for a rash on her arm: "She is in strict purdah & was clad in a curious hooded gown with only two little peepholes for her eyes. As she had a rash on her face as well, I told him I could not prescribe without seeing the lesions there. So she was told to come out from her extraordinary garment & a rather grubby

but fairly young apparition appeared in the light of day. Aren't
their habits curious?"

It is easy to see Bernard as a somewhat Blimpish figure,
adopting all the mannerisms and attitudes of the colonial over-
lords, but he was a little more complicated than that. Although
convinced of the British duty to see to the welfare of the be-
nighted Indian who was as yet incapable of taking care of himself, he had a sharp eye for the theatrical aspects of the imperial
ethos.

On July 6, 1942, Bernard has just been to a reception given
by the viceroy to celebrate the independence of the United
States, which seems a very strange thing to do in the heart of
the British Empire. The viceroy at the time was Lord Linlithgow, a deeply reactionary figure who did his utmost to stifle
any Indian demands for independence. But no doubt the celebration of American independence was a way to be nice to the
much-needed Yankee allies, adding one more absurdity to a
rich supply of late imperial farces. The celebration was at the
viceregal house in New Delhi, in Bernard's words "a vast edifice built in light terracotta and white stone with a high round
black dome affair on top. The building is well-proportioned
and fits in well with all the rest of the official New Delhi designed by Lutyens, although I must confess it has a certain
Wembley Exhibition* air about it . . . Everything is built on a
vast scale no doubt to impress the Oriental mind." A buffet was

---

*He is referring to the British Empire Exhibition held at Wembley in 1925, to
celebrate with a great deal of pomp the glories of the British Raj. Sir Edward
Elgar, as "Master of the King's Musick," composed the *Empire March* especially
for the occasion.

laid out in a room with "portraits of all the past Viceroys, mostly painted by Oswald Birley, but one or two by de Laszlo. That of Reading was I thought the most striking."

It is interesting that he would say that. Lord Reading, depicted in all his imperial pomp by Philip de László, a Hungarian-born Jewish society painter in England, was the first and only Jewish viceroy of India. His name was Rufus Isaacs, described by his great-grandson Simon Isaacs as "a liberal Jew" who "was more English than he was Jewish."

This was not quite Bernard's milieu; he would have found it pretentious. The picture of Lord Reading looking very lordly in his long-legged cream-coloured trousers and wearing the light blue velvet cape of the Grand Master of the Star of India reminded me of a much earlier letter from Bernard, which I neglected to quote. It was written on September 21, 1924, when he was scouting around southern England with his medical superiors for a suitable place to establish a convalescent home. They go around various grand country houses and are received by the owners for tea. Bernard describes entering a vast oak-panelled hall, just the sort of place one would have found de László portraits hanging on the wall. He writes to Win, "This is Captain so & so, may I introduce you to Lady Thingamebob— you know the style and I felt like the arch villain in a modern shilling shocker."

On August 1, 1942, a month after attending the viceroy's reception to celebrate American independence, and a week before the Indian Congress Party began its Quit India rebellion against the British Raj, Bernard has dinner with an Indian sur-

geon at the Indian Military Hospital. Bernard writes, "After a
while he thawed somewhat and although not anti-British he
opened his heart about the colour question. His life had certainly been complicated by his having married an English wife
from whom he is now divorced. It was an interesting session."

Quite where Bernard stood in this matter is unclear. I know
that he had been sceptical about mixed marriages. When one
of the hostel children, Lore Feig, decided to marry a Parsee
after the war, Bernard advised her against it, not because he
disapproved of Parsees, but because he feared that social com-
plications made such marriages too risky. He didn't object, so
far as I know, to his daughter marrying my father, who was
from a Protestant family, but perhaps in his eyes a marriage
between Europeans did not count as mixed. His mother,
known to me as Great Grandma, worried a little about having
a Dutchman in the family, since he might, she worried, have
had a drop of "Indonesian blood."

The Anglo-Russian philosopher Isaiah Berlin liked to tell a
story about the distinguished British historian Lewis Namier,
born in Russia as Ludwik Niemirowski. Sometime in the 1930s,
a visitor from Nazi Germany held forth at an Oxford dinner
about the validity of German territorial demands in Europe,
which he compared to the righteousness of the British Empire,
whereupon Namier growled, "We Jews and other coloured
peoples think otherwise," and stomped out.

I'm not sure what Bernard would have made of Namier's
remark. I doubt very much that he would have ranked himself
among the coloured peoples, but the vulnerability of his own

status in British society and his basic humanity shielded him from the contempt that some of his British cohorts felt for the people they still, however tenuously, continued to rule. He often felt that Indian politeness put European "boorishness" to shame. To which Win replies on December 1, 1943, "That feeling of boorishness, in the face of fine manners and ceremony towards guests of the Indians, I remember so well in my relations with Kamala Sircar at college. She always seemed far too gentle and delicate in her manners for the rough and ready methods of the undergrads."

While Bernard was sending Win accounts of his encounters with Indians, she was fretting about her domestic problems. Life in the English countryside was made difficult by strict rations of petrol and food. On March 4, when Bernard was still on board his ship, she writes about the various disasters in the Far East: "Singapore gone, the Dutch East Indies practically finished, alas, after their brave fight . . . Things indeed look depressing at the moment." She then goes into a long description of the garden at Mount Pleasant, the fate of the vegetables, the pea seeds, the state of the apple orchard, and the latest cut in food rations. She "tactfully" suggested to Laura "how we could harbour our resources here and there against the approaching lean times." This apparently angered Laura, who seemed to regard it as Win's personal meanness. "Really," Win declares, "some of the working classes have no idea of sacrifice or war effort at all."

Then there was Hall, the gardener, who was lazy and often obstructive, according to Win. Indeed, she writes on Septem-

Laura at Mount Pleasant

ber 13 that "he has become Bolshy,* and told Laura, in Hilary's hearing, that he hoped when the revolution came the rich would be shot up!!"

Such outbursts were rare, however. On the whole Win's relations with the "working classes" in her employment were warm, even intimate in the way class relations based on mutual dependence often were. The same letter, quoted above, about the politesse of her Indian friend at Oxford, rather gushes about the staff. Laura, she writes, "is a treasure & she lives with

---

*"Bolshy" or "Bolshie" is derived from "Bolshevik," but came to mean a person who was obstructive or disruptive.

her whole being for us & our children. Her thoughts are continually with you & she is as excited as I am when news comes from you . . . She is looking after me most tenderly & devotedly, and what I should do without her, I don't know. She has drawn Mr. May and Mrs. Tuttle into the family devotion, so that Mr. May refers to me as 'our missus.'"

Mr. "Bill" May is only a name to me. Laura was evidently keen on him, but he died young in a car crash. Mrs. Tuttle, who did the cleaning, I do remember as a thin and very old woman with one dark brown tooth left in her mouth. We would visit her from time to time at a tiny cottage near Newbury where she lived alone in Dickensian squalor. We never stayed for long.

Living with domestic help, which was the normal condition of the upper middle class, even in a country cottage, was not without problems. But if the help sometimes got on Win's nerves, her children were worse. On September 9, she writes that they "are desperately out of hand; I cut no ice at all & I know now that I've failed with them. They are all lazy to a degree, even Wendy, and the others are rude and defiant into the bargain. Not one of them is sufficiently public-spirited to wish to do anything for the country . . . I am afraid, having been brought up as they were, with a staff of servants & a nurse & governess, it is too late now to make them anything but soft and selfish."

If only she could see the end of the world's miseries, but the news was so grim and *The Times* was predicting a ten years' war: "Shall we ever meet again, my dear, or have we had all the life together for which we were destined?"

The refuge from her troubles, her safe haven, as it were,

apart from her music, was that most English of institutions, her garden, which she tended with deep devotion. I can still picture her bent over the flowerbeds at St. Mary Woodlands, pruning and hoeing and weeding for hours on end. Even as the news about battlefronts and murderous persecution was getting worse all the time, she still managed to worry about the state of her garden. On July 11, 1941, she writes about the Mount Pleasant garden that "the borders are a riot of colour and the lavender magnificent, but nothing is staked up or properly attended to." A week later, on the fifteenth, she reports that things are improving in the kitchen garden, but she has not yet had time to tackle the flower garden, which is "a complete shambles." Gifford will be coming to stay, she writes, and "I don't know what [he] will think of it."

Her garden in Hampstead had been affected less by the Blitz, it appears, than by Win's absence. The German relatives, who lived there through the war, lacked her enthusiasm and diligence in this regard. The sight of the garden in Templewood Avenue, she reports on July 4, 1943, made her "weep with sorrow." It was so sad "to think that so young and beautiful a garden could revert to such a state in so short a time. No English inhabitants would have allowed it to get like that."

This might strike one as overwrought, even slightly unhinged in the midst of a war. But the state of Win's garden, no less than the clothes she wore, or the manners of her children, was of huge importance to her. For it was intimately connected to her perception of her place in the world, and to the way others perceived her. And these others included people from all classes. She would change out of her gardening clothes just to pick someone up at the village station, lest the stationmaster see her in anything but the most respectable attire.

I can't remember who told us the story of Win's behaviour at some smart dinner party in London. Perhaps it was Win herself. A careless mistake had been made in the kitchen. Instead of a bowl of custard for dessert, Win had been served a bowl of mayonnaise. She finished it up to the last spoonful, without a word of complaint.

On July 17, 1942, Bernard mentions a meeting in Delhi with the Duke of Gloucester, brother of King George VI. It was during a reception for Indian doctors at the residence of the military commander in chief, Archibald Wavell, described by Bernard as a small man with a "tight little mouth." Bernard is "called up to make conversation with the Duke. He told me that he had lost all his peas and beans with the frost two months ago in England."

To which Win replies more than a month later, on August 21, "I was amused by your gardening chat with the Duke. Gardening, as I long ago discovered, is the British 'open sesame' to all doors & seldom fails in any walk of life." It was an insight, perhaps, that would not have been put in quite those terms by someone who had never felt the need to open doors, or feared having them closed in her face.

But there was more to the gardening fetish than that. I have already quoted Bernard's letter about Mount Pleasant being his "idyll" of "home and England." He elaborates on this theme in a letter sent on March 4, 1943. Inspired by Win's description of the Kintbury garden and of "glorious Berkshire," he launches into a romantic rhapsody about their shared country idyll: "I have been in many countries & seen many of the glories of nature with you, beloved. Recently I have become acquainted with some of the beauties of this country here. Somehow, though, nowhere will really ever hold comparison to the simple peaceful loveliness of our English countryside . . . Berkshire. Whenever I write it on your letters it gives me a thrill . . . Darling I am feasting my eyes once again on my loving and gallant little lady with her decks cleared for action in the garden, capacious pockets in her apron, a gardening fork almost as big as herself, great gloves . . . How I would love to see it all again and dig my spade into the good Berkshire soil." And so on.

It is hard to imagine, reading these bursts of sentiment about the earth of home, that Bernard and Win had lived for most of their lives in north-west London. Bernard had spent less than two years altogether in Berkshire. The quest for a safe haven explains his feelings to some degree. Similarly lyrical passages occur in his letters about Hohfluh, the Swiss village, and the Hotel Wagram in Paris. Still, I think the paeans to the Berkshire soil were about more than a sense of security; they expressed a desire to be embedded in the idyll, proof, contrary to what some bigots believe, that no one clings more tenaciously to newly planted roots than the patriotic immigrant or his offspring, on condition, of course, that they feel accepted.

Ten days after Bernard wrote his love letter to the Berkshire countryside from the British Military Hospital in Delhi, the roughly forty-five thousand Jews of Salonika, where Bernard had been stationed in the previous war, were being deported to

Auschwitz-Birkenau. Most were gassed as soon as they arrived.
By the time his letter reached Win, the uprising in the Warsaw
Ghetto had begun. But by then, millions of European Jews had
already been slaughtered, machine-gunned into slimy pits, or
gassed in the main killing centres in Poland. Many people,
including Jews who spent the war in relative safety in Britain or
the United States, would claim after the war that they hadn't
known how bad things had been. Perhaps for most people it
was beyond their imagination. Win was not one of those
people.

Her letter of September 28, 1942, begins in a normal manner, informing Bernard about the Christmas presents on the
way to him in Delhi, a pipe he had asked for, packed along with
ten volumes of Charles Dickens. Roger's progress at his prep
school is mentioned, how well he was doing at sports and his
keenness as a cricketer. A weekend visit to Mount Pleasant by
Gifford is announced; she hopes he won't be too frightfully
bored by her company and expects him to help her in the garden. She is rehearsing Bach's *Peasant Cantata* with Gerald
Finzi's chamber orchestra for a concert.

This is how the letter ends: "Such terribly sad news comes
from Holland and Germany. You have probably heard that Bernard Schuster, his wife & Steffi's son[*] have been deported, &
that nothing is known of them. Today Lotte Levy[†] writes that
her poor mother, who has been a frail invalid for years, has
been deported from Germany (that probably means gassed

---

[*]Relatives on Bernard's side.
[†]The mother of Hans Levy.

or shot!). Edith Rosenzweig's mother has met a similar fate. Lotte's sister & brother-in-law have recently 'died' in concentration camp."

Bernard does not receive this letter until the end of December. There is no comment on the horrifying news. What could he possibly say? Instead, on December 24, he tries to imagine being at home: "Christmas Eve & my thoughts are with you all at Kintbury where great preparations must be in progress. I can picture the decorations round the walls probably left to John's tender care again, trays to prepare, stockings to fill, last minute cards to be despatched & all the rest of the paraphernalia associated with this annual festivity. How I would like to mount my Grane & appear among you as a surprise in time for that very early morning call of the children on Christmas day."

The only eccentric detail in this sentimental Christmas card imagery is the mention of Grane, the horse ridden by Brünnhilde into the flames in Wagner's *Twilight of the Gods*. But for Bernard, this was not peculiar at all; Wagner's *Ring* was as close to his Jewish heart as Christmas Eve, perhaps even more so. Both Bernard and Win were keen to distance themselves from their German family origins. But music was different—when the Bayreuth Festival, so deeply tainted not only by Wagner's own anti-Semitism but by Hitler's frequent attendance, was resumed in the early 1950s, the entire Schlesinger family travelled there to celebrate the rebirth of Wagner's Teutonic shrine.

While having a German background had been a clear liability in World War I, being Jewish was obviously a more sensitive issue in World War II. It made Bernard and Win more ferociously anti-German. But it also complicated the ways in which they saw, or chose to declare, their place in the world. Bernard's attitude was best summed up in a letter sent from Northern Ireland on September 7, 1941: "Acting on the principle that one should let people get to know you first & then, if you get on with them, to do one's racial apostolic act, I enlightened the Martins the other night and early morning during a long and earnest conversation over a protracted cup of tea."

And yet their sense of solidarity with other Jews did not entirely dispel certain prejudices they had absorbed from the world they had chosen to live in. Win wrote on October 13, 1941, that "personally" she was "happy & equally at home in the company of any human being, be he duke or railway porter." This was true up to a point. It was perhaps even truer of Bernard, but when it came to Jews, they had their own ideas on how people ought to behave. Or put it this way: they were easily embarrassed by Jews, perhaps in the way upper-middle-class people are often pained to see their less refined compatriots disporting themselves in tourist spots.

In August 1943, Win takes a train back to Kintbury from a family holiday in Wales. After a change of trains at Birmingham, she writes on September 1 that they shared a compartment "with a very Jewish-looking gentleman & his wife. He was a barrister who knew Walter quite well. He was rather typical of his race, with the oriental disdain of women's intellect. He offered Roger his newspaper—being the only man in the carriage besides himself, as he put it, and he addressed all his more intelligent conversation to Roger, reserving poor jokes for the mere females."

I am sure he was insufferable, but "rather typical of his

race" is a strange thing to say, especially at a time of murderous persecution. Win's remark dropped in a letter on October 4 is even more revealing. Vera Baer, one of the hostel children, had sent Win a letter, "enclosing a charming little photograph of herself. She has grown into a very pretty young girl, without a trace of 45 or German." *Without a trace of 45?* This was more than Win could say of herself, or indeed any of her kin. More than once, she frets about my mother Wendy's perfectly respectable Jewish nose. A minimum of 45, combined with a thorough "de-Germanization," was clearly essential to gain her approval.

Bernard comes across some "45s" in India too. At the military club in Agra, in September 1943, he dines with the Holmans, "forty-five, he with Australian antecedents & she with I should think Polish or Russian." Dr. Holman did rather well in the Burma campaign and "got a mention for it." Bernard certainly approves of this. Holman, he writes, is "a good type of 45," a "Maccabean" even. Besides these martial qualities, he "is a man of ambition & ideas rather typical of his race." That expression again. I'm not quite sure what he means, but I have a suspicion it is not wholly positive.

Reading on, in the correspondence of 1944, the question of Dr. Holman's ideas becomes, like Alice's experiences in Wonderland, "curiouser and curiouser." Holman, Bernard writes on August 10, 1944, "is a small man with big ideas for future generations and seriously wants his wife to have a selected child via the Eugenic Society." This from a Jew at the time of the Shoah! Bernard: "I think he is mad & she likewise for even attempting to agree."

Indeed, but *eugenics*, typical of the Jewish race?

A year later, on December 12, 1944, Bernard writes about dining in the company of Indian medical officers and one specialist "who is a pleasant & knowledgeable German refugee, now a captain in the RAMC by the name of Habisch—shades of the *Ring*. He is one of the best types, quiet and a credit to his race, inspiring confidence in these rather ultra English military men whose regiments he has to doctor."

Quiet, not too openly Jewish, with military backbone, able to reassure the ultra-Englishmen—these were the cardinal virtues. And Bernard, though loud of voice (but not of manner), and not at all without ambition for himself or his family, including his grandchildren, certainly managed to live up to the second requirement. He was a Maccabean to the core.

After more than a year of living apart on different continents, certain worries started to creep into the correspondence, despite the constant expressions of their deepest devotion to one another. Win was still in her mid-forties, but she was concerned about getting old while Bernard was "gallivanting" or "swanning" about, as she put it more than once. Would she still be attractive to him when they were finally reunited? Or would their vastly different experiences make them drift apart?

In a letter from Mount Pleasant on October 25, 1942, Win reminds him of the "hayricks, all neatly thatched," of "the fields glowing from an extra rich green from the moisture," of "the hedges full of berries," of "the hips and haws, & shiny black privet and dogwood—And there is your Berkshire for

Win at Mount Pleasant

you!" Inside the same envelope was a photograph of her, taken by Laura. She is standing in the garden, smiling, a shovel in her left hand, a dog at her feet. "Not very beautiful," she writes, "but I'm afraid it's what I look like now." She has let her hair grow "as being more becoming to a rapidly ageing matron." Darling, she continues, "when you take me in your arms again for the first time, I feel that I should then perhaps rejuvenate a little again, from the feeling of your warm love. Now I always feel half starved, and that is a bad & unbecoming condition."

A month before this, on September 23, things looked even grimmer; a rare note of recrimination darkens her prose, as though her feeling of abandonment were Bernard's fault: "I find it hard to write now, as there is no response from you at all, & I feel you have lost interest in us here, & we have begun to lose touch already . . . I feel terribly alone in the world now; there is plenty of work and responsibility, but seldom a change or a gay moment . . . You managed to write daily to your parents in the last war because they demanded it from you; I demand nothing, but my request is much more modest than that, & I think even more important."

She had to wait at least three months for an answer, even though a few airgraphs would have got through in the meantime. He received her letter only on December 2 and writes back the next day, from Delhi: "I can understand your sense of desolation & apprehension at our apparent endless separation & the prospect of your having to deal with your ever increasing domestic and family problems unaided. Added to that you feared I was forgetting you . . . You must never let such a thought ever worry you again. You & your life & our home & our family are constantly on my mind."

Bernard feels guilty about his "relatively comfortable existence" compared to her "very largely drab life." He thinks it is "all wrong." He "should be stuck somewhere in the desert in the middle of things and then our respective jobs and enforced separated mode of existence would again be in the right perspective."

Instead, he is often stuck in Delhi or Agra, dealing with the administration and inspection of Indian and British military hospitals, playing squash, dining at the club, riding in the early mornings, attending dances, acting as father confessor to the unhappy wives of military and medical colleagues. Here in front of me are the photographs of his children holding their various musical instruments, in leather frames stuck together like a concertina that could be unfolded and proudly displayed on the mantelpiece of his office. Bernard would later describe them as "the straight and narrow," supposed to keep him from the natural temptations that would afflict any man condemned to be on his own, or indeed any small community of bored expatriates stranded far from home.

There is no evidence that Bernard ever strayed from the straight and narrow himself. To describe his enforced bachelor life, he fell back on his usual metaphors drawn from literature and Wagner's operas. Rudyard Kipling had always been one of his favourite authors. My own potential enjoyment of Kipling was hampered for life ever since Bernard insisted on reading his stories to me when I was too young to appreciate them. Even *The Jungle Book* failed to pique my interest when I was five or six. In the summer of 1943, Bernard had decided to re-read *Kim* "in the light of what I've seen now in this country," as well as *Plain Tales from the Hills*, featuring, among other memorable characters, Mrs. Hauksbee, who chewed on her riding whip when she was thinking.

On June 13, 1943, from the Akbar Barracks in Agra, Bernard writes, "Here I should judge that general morals have changed little since the days of Mrs. Hawksby [*sic*]. I never cease to wonder & shudder a little at the entanglements matrimonial and otherwise that go on out here—a bad place for a Parsifalian lad like myself, but have no fear—no Kundrys for me—just my own beloved Win to look up to. I am glad I love you so much—it makes life so very much easier."

Kundry was the wild and tormented woman of mystery sent to seduce the pure naïve Parsifal and divert him from redeeming the knights of the holy grail. The notion of Bernard as the pure Parsifal saving the grail from which Christ sipped at the Last Supper is interesting. At the same time, it would have astonished him to hear that Kundry, according to some commentators, was an anti-Semitic caricature of the Jewish seductress. Bernard's Wagnerian imagination was a bit like his (and Win's) English patriotism: they chose to see what they saw, and ignored the disturbing bits.

Wagner pops up in the most unexpected places. In August of the same year, Bernard embarked on a trek through Kashmir with two "coolie-bearer-guides," one old cook with a dyed red beard "who knows his stuff," eight ponies, and a number of "pony wallahs." It was the kind of experience he relished, bathing in ice-cold rivers, picking fresh walnuts from the trees, and sleeping under the stars. The only thing he missed in the Himalayan Hills was the company of his wife. Writing by the light of a hurricane lamp on the night of August 21, he says, "As the sun set, one end of the valley with its rather green hills & light clouds looked like the opening stages of the 'Ring' and I almost expected Fafner and Fasolt* to appear before Wotan & the remainder of the gods, while at the opposite end, the rather rugged sinister rocky mountains with the sun's waning light reminded me of the last act of 'Gotterdämmerung' & I waited to see Walhalla go up in flames any minute in the distance and

---

*Fafner, who is later transformed into a dragon, and his brother Fasolt promise Wotan that they will build Valhalla in exchange for the goddess Freya.

Brünnhilde mounted on her white steeds riding to her destruction. It's been a grand day walking through this happy valley
through rice fields and past all the wild flowers that grow
in the English countryside."

So here we have it: Wagner's Valhalla with the sweet odours
of England.

One of Bernard's duties was to inspect the military hospitals of
northern India, all the way to the border of Afghanistan. To
amuse Win, he recounts some of his adventures. On the way to
Srinagar in Kashmir, he visits a lunatic asylum and reports on
March 26, 1943, "The superintendent is one of those Indians
who seem to regard life as rather a joke—I know the type so
well now—and so, as he took me round, problems and difficulties that I mentioned as possibly arising in his particular work
dissolved into a chuckle and a contented shrug of the shoulders
on his part. He is a good man in many ways to be at the head of
an asylum."

Together they watch a man who has lectured to an empty
room for the last twenty years. Bernard observes that what he
has to say does not seem entirely unreasonable.

In a station near Agra, in April, he looks up an old school-
mate from Uppingham. They used to collaborate on exams in
history and divinity. His name is Dyer, now Major Dyer in the
regular army. A keen violinist, Major Dyer was just playing the
Brahms Violin Concerto on his gramophone when Bernard arrived, bringing back many pleasant memories. Major Dyer happened to be the son of Reginald Dyer, the man who, fearing an

Indian rebellion, massacred more than a thousand unarmed civilians in Amritsar in 1919. "So much for Dyer," writes Bernard on April 3.

He visits the famous Residency in Lucknow, which, he writes on June 6, "stands in grim ruins with the Union Jack flying steadfastly on its tower flagstaff. Here was made the famous stand against the Mutiny in 1857 when close to 3000 were invested for six months—soldiers, women & children . . . It was about here that the march sings 'The Campbells are coming, Hurrah, Hurrah.'"

On the North-West Frontier, he meets Pathans. The Pathan, he declares on August 20, "takes life much more as a joke but is often thoroughly untrustworthy. He is also said to have peculiar habits which we don't consider very nice."

Bernard's political opinions on India are cautious and on the whole absent from his letters to Win. When she asks him what he thinks of the appointment of Field Marshal Wavell as the new viceroy of India, he answers, in the same letter quoted above, that he is a good choice. "An Indian Viceroy would be quite impossible with the existing Hindu-Muslim rivalry, apart from any other consideration and these are manifold . . . The reaction of the Indian soldiers to the appointment is good. The average Indian civilian is, shall we say, I should think resigned."

Quite who is the "average Indian civilian" remains a bit hazy. But Bernard's report of an encounter with "a young civilian Mahomedan" in March 1944 makes it clear that the end of the British Raj, and even the way it would end, was already a common topic of discussion. On March 18, Bernard is on an overnight train to Agra. The Muslim, an engineer, shares his carriage. They engage in a long discussion. "His politics," writes Bernard, "were interesting. He thought the British should clear out, even though he said it would almost certainly mean civil war. In the same breath, he spoke about improved economic conditions for the Indians, little heeding that the one would postpone the other indefinitely. The Hindus outnumber the Musulmen by 3 to 1, and the latter are frightened that their interests would never be served if representatives in the central national Government were in that proportion. So they want a trial of strength as to who should have the power. He agreed that this was not an ideal manner of beginning a new regime but had no other solution. What's to be done with a country which thinks in these terms and he is a well educated man?"

Wavell was directly involved in the most dramatic event during Bernard's time in India. A famine in 1943 caused the deaths by starvation, malnutrition, or disease of roughly three million Bengalis. The reasons are still disputed. A cyclone in January destroyed many rice crops. Government statistics on food production were highly unreliable. The Japanese occupation of Burma cut off rice supplies. The hugely expanded Indian army needed to be fed. Provincial governments were often corrupt and refused to divert food to other parts of India. Lord Linlithgow, the viceroy before Wavell, was convinced that there was no shortage in Bengal and that people were simply hoarding rice and grain. Some historians blame Winston Churchill, who blocked shipments of grain to Bengal because the "sturdy Greeks," who were also going hungry, were more in need, in Churchill's view, than the wretched Bengalis.

Much of the news on the famine was allegedly suppressed

in Britain. But it was Win, in a letter sent on November 18, when the hunger was most acute, who brought it up. Her main concern was Bernard himself: "Are you affected by the famine trouble in Bengal, although it is not your district? For heaven's sake take precautions against cholera and other diseases."

Bernard answered a month later in an airgraph, dated December 15. "Yes," he writes, "the Bengal mess is certainly tragic. I read the Indian minister of food's statement in the assembly. Most has to do with provincial lack of cooperation, a weak governor & the normal Indian's absence of charity from his character. Much [unreadable] has gone on at the unfortunate starving multitudes' expense."

Bernard might have mentioned a lack of charity on Churchill's part too, but that would not have occurred to him. Churchill was the epitome of everything he and Win admired.

When General Wavell took over as viceroy from the hopeless Linlithgow in the summer of 1943, this inspired a peculiarly optimistic letter from Bernard, written on October 31, when the famine was still raging in Bengal. "Good old Wavell," he writes. "It needed a soldier to wake up the slow-moving & ineffective Provincial Indian legislature & take active steps to put an end to all the misery in Bengal."

He was not wrong. Lord Wavell did open up reserves of grain and soon after the new year the worst would be over. There was more good news, not least on the Eastern Front, where German armies had been routed at Stalingrad and Kursk: "Amazing these Russians are," writes Bernard, "and we are not doing badly. I read a good address which [General] Montgomery sent to his old prep school . . . in which he explains how N. Africa & the campaign in the Mid East & Sicily, etc. had been the turning point of the war. Win, do you think we dare to hope that the Bosch will be defeated in the early part of 1944 & the Japs at the end of it. I still have visions of Christmas at Mount Pleasant in 1944."

Win, as always, is less easily buoyed up. She feels that their forced separation might be a kind of punishment. December 8, 1943: "Perhaps we were too happy, too secure in our great love & our comfortable circumstances."

She could not face the new year without feeling deeply worried. John was now almost old enough to be called up. On December 26, Boxing Day, when the whole family except Bernard is gathered around the Christmas tree in Mount Pleasant, Win writes, "My heart bleeds to realise that the day is drawing ever nearer, when [John] too must leave me to plunge into this devilish vortex. I dare not look into the future, & can only half-heartedly join in the merry chatter about future plans and hopes, because at the back of my mind there is always that secret dread: 'Is there going to be a future?'"

Eight

THE BEGINNING
OF THE END

—·—

W in had said it before, but never quite as succinctly as on March 2, 1943: "Today, while I was gardening, a time when many thoughts and philosophies run through my mind—I said to myself there are just two things in this world which make me proud and eternally thankful. One is that I am an English woman, privileged to live in and for the most wonderful country in the world, and the other is that I won the unique and faithful love of such a man as you."

Reassured that the family would almost certainly be spared a fate that was still easy to imagine a year or two before, Win's patriotism was boosted even more by her gratitude. It was boundless: not only had England not rejected her in the way that Germany had done to her own relatives, but she felt strongly that England had saved the lives of her family. Which was why she couldn't really abide people who didn't share the same feelings. When one of the hostel children, Peter Hecht, hopes to go to university to study medicine, and expects Bernard and Win to pay for his further education, she writes, on January 1, 1944, that this is out of the question. He lacks the ability, there isn't the money, and "I also reminded him that he owes a debt to England before he thinks of his own future."

But there were limits even to Win's readiness to suffer for her country, let alone its empire. When E. M. Forster said that given the choice between betraying his friend or his country, he hoped he would have the guts to betray his country, he spoke as a humanist. Personal loyalty should be valued more highly than loyalty to an abstraction. Some might say that "country" is not an abstraction, especially when it has to be defended against a mortal danger. Win would no doubt have thought that. But personal considerations tempered even her patriotic zeal.

In May 1940, when she heard that Bernard would be pulled out of Narvik, she wrote that her country was worth more than her private happiness, more even than Bernard's return, which, if necessary, had to be postponed for England's honour.

I don't think she would have put it quite like that four years later. Win was so desperate for Bernard to come home that she worried about his desire to embark on more dangerous duties than inspecting military hospitals in northern India. On January 11, 1944, she writes, "I know your fear, which is almost a fetish, of appearing unpatriotic or un-public spirited, but . . . you would apply for a return to England, wouldn't you, when you are legally entitled to it?"

Bernard taking it easy

Who was more fetishistic in this regard, Bernard or Win, is hard to say. But Bernard's desire for more action had been there from the beginning of the war. He was restless at Benenden, bored in Ormskirk and Bangor, and felt guilty about his hectic but relatively shielded existence in India. In September 1942, he writes about having to give away one of his hospital nurses at her wedding. He hopes he won't have to wear a sword for the occasion, for fear of tripping over it: "What false peacetime soldiering, it all seems to be here," he grumbles.

Was this just an excess of patriotic zeal, as Win's letter suggests? I don't think so. The frustration goes deeper. Bernard explains himself in more detail on January 12, 1943, after commiserating with Win's difficulties in keeping the household going under increasingly harsh material constraints. "I feel ashamed," Bernard writes, "when I'm faced with the good things out here & am beginning to feel more and more my war morale being sapped by the fleshpots. It was mainly for that reason that I vainly sought a transfer to greater trials & discomforts for the good of my soul."

There can't have been many people in 1943 who actively pined for greater hardships. For most it was hard enough to survive, and for most Jews in Europe even that was impossible. But the more Bernard heard about the miseries in Europe, or even in England, which was still incomparably better off than countries under German occupation, the more uneasy he felt about his life as an officer of the British Raj. His shock at the squalor and inequality of Indian society added to his sense of guilt. Not that he blamed such conditions on the Empire itself; on the contrary, lifting India from its own wretchedness was, for him, and others like him, a justification for continued British rule.

Here he is in Naini Tal, a pleasant hill station in the Himalayas, famous for its grand views of snowy mountains, and sailing on the lake, for which the British, in Bernard's words on June 3, 1944, "dress up for the part, complete with yachting caps, blue tops & white flannels on Sunday morning." Cars are not allowed to disturb the peace up there among the summer villas and municipal buildings in the "domestic Gothic" style. Rickshaws, "pulled and pushed up the steep hills by four coolies at a trot," are the only form of transport for the sahibs and memsahibs on their way to the tennis courts and tea parties. Bernard feels guilty about this too, "as I think it's undignified for people to be hauled about by their fellow men acting as beasts of burden . . . Only once have I travelled in one in Simla, soon after I came out & then I helped them push up the steep bits instead of being a passenger—they thought I was quite mad & feared I would not pay them at the end."

India often disgusted him. It was a country, he writes on August 1, "where there has always been one law for the wealthy & a very different one for the common herd & I fear this will never change, Quit India or no." Sometimes the squalor of India, the beggars, the constant tang of poverty overwhelmed him. Taking a stroll around the station at Cawnpore one day while waiting for his next train, he observes children defecating in the streets of "the native quarters," which "we practically always miss in our rapid transport to the Cantonments from the railway station," the flies, the stink, the open sores: "What a country!"

Back on the train, he opens an old copy of *Country Life*, the type of magazine from the home country that would have been piled up on the side tables in the officers' mess or the golf club at any colonial outpost. Reading *Country Life* on the train, he writes on January 16, "wafts away these Oriental smells & gives me the feeling of cleanliness again with its pictures of sunny, bright and verdant England, smiling and friendly, with its fine stately old mansions, undulating plough land, woods, birdlife, country lore, queries and answers about the pleasant things in life—habits, customs, antiquities, collector's pieces, articles on husbandry, fruit trees & daffodils. There, I feel better now, as if a draught of fresh air had blown through my bones."

This was the sentimental vision of home cultivated by many British servants of the Empire, who only later found themselves much too late in life, after years in the tropical sun, miserable and isolated in some rain-sodden village in the Home Counties. Bernard, too, pined for his safe haven, his Berkshire idyll, but what he wanted at the same time was to be tested in action, be it against Japanese or Germans, preferably the latter, as long as he no longer had to feel in danger of going soft in body and soul.

Win understood his feelings, although she often assumed, only half in jest, that he was swanning about town with "young damsels" while she was growing old and ugly waiting for him to come home. He continuously had to reassure her on this score. But she was alarmed by his restlessness. She didn't even like him flying around India on airplanes, after she read reports of regular plane crashes in that country.

If Bernard was tugged by mixed desires—for going home as well as for the ruggedness of combat—her feelings were no less contradictory. For she admired his gung-ho attitude in spite of her anxiety, and couldn't help comparing her husband's manliness to what she saw as the lack of it in her eldest son. Even as Bernard is hungry for action, John is on his summer holiday in Kintbury preparing to appear as Carmen Miranda in a variety show he put together. This is his last year at Uppingham. His school career has not been a success. Win reports with a modicum of pride that at least he had a part in the school play ("female inevitably"), which he seems to "have carried off outstandingly well." His head is filled with movies he has seen, plays attended (John Gielgud and Laurence Olivier at the Old Vic), and plans for future shows when he goes up to Oxford. But before Oxford, he will have to serve in the army, a prospect that horrifies him and alarms Win.

Win to Bernard, February 23, 1943, about John: "He is such a kind, clean honest fellow, and in so many ways still so refreshingly ingenuous, and so good-natured, but he is utterly lazy, spineless & self-centred. My great fear is that if he should become actively involved in this war, he will fail to lead his men into battle with courage and determination."

Win's attitude, expressed in different tones and variations over and over in her letters, is that of many mothers in times of war. She wants John to do his duty for his country. She wants him to be brave, to lead his men into battle. She even thinks the army might "do him some good." Bernard agrees. Even though John has his mind set on "the stage and set designing," he writes on February 2, 1944, "no doubt the forthcoming army life will have settled his ideas along more orthodox and safer lines by the time he is through with it."

What she cannot understand is how they, Bernard and Win, "who have always been rather exceptionally energetic and public spirited come by children like John and Wendy." My mother, too, was evidently a disappointment, even though her proficiency with the cello redeemed her a bit. Whereas John could think of nothing else but the theatre: "He doesn't sleep when he has a show on."

The most remarkable letter of all, on John's manliness, or the lack of it, was written by Win after the war against Germany was already won and there was still a chance of her son being sent to fight the Japanese. He has failed hopelessly in military training as a common soldier in the Royal Engineers and is laid up for weeks, possibly for psychosomatic reasons, at a hospital in Manchester. She is responding to a letter sent by

Bernard on June 6, 1945, where he mentions the possibility of having John transferred to ENSA, the army entertainment division. That is indeed where he ended up, happily putting on drag shows for the troops in Singapore with Kenneth Williams and Peter Nichols, who later dramatized this experience in a musical play entitled *Privates on Parade*. Bernard is less hard on John than is Win, and reminds her of his own mental deterioration in 1918—"perhaps you think that I have never really recovered from then & you may be right."

Win replies on the sixteenth (the mail had improved by then) that John has become "mentally and physically flabby. No comparison with yourself in 1915–18, who were an active soldier in the field, doing very much a man's job. If I had thought you mentally or physically flabby I shouldn't have married you."

This admirably expressed her love for Bernard, but it was also an extraordinary thing to say, pitting her artistic son against his heartier father, as though the former would always be found wanting. There is, however, an element of bluff in her pugnacious talk, for much as she might have deplored her son's flabbiness, she was also terrified of losing him. Pride and terror are the two faces of the war mother. But Win is no mother of Coriolanus, who bullies her son into becoming a warrior. When she thinks there is a real danger of John actually having to fight, she is petrified. In March 1944, the much-dreaded letter arrives in Kintbury from the War Office, ordering John to Liverpool for a crash course as a soldier in the Royal Engineers.

On March 27, Win appears to have forgotten her disappointment with John's lack of machismo: "They want to bring these youngsters through their training as quickly as possible to provide more cannon fodder for the Japs. Poor John! He is so very young and immature. I pray to God that he may be equal to whatever is before him. I'm afraid I do not make a good soldier's wife & mother. My heart is so heavy, and my imagination is too active."

In answer to this letter, on April 12, Bernard doesn't comment on John's prospects in the army, but does mention that John has written to him and "opened out more than he ever has done to me before & I was touched." He praises his son as "a young man of some spiritual thought and certainly with a very strong family sense." Bernard is also relieved to hear that John has a girlfriend, Betty Hall, a friend of Wendy's from Badminton School, not Jewish, which is all right, for Bernard has "long got over my prejudice against mixed entanglements, although on the whole I believe two of a kind make for greater and more solid happiness."

Betty was evidently mad about John. Win thinks they are "very much in love." But she is reassured by her son's innocence in sexual matters, greater, she assumes, than that of his younger brother, Roger, who was observed kissing a young "sex-starved" nurse on the lips. Win on January 19, 1944: "I don't think we need to worry too much about the boys' amatory excursions—certainly not about John's. He is an awfully clean chap, & thinks the most harmless remarks wicked and daring!"

Anyone who knew John later in life would find this an astounding statement. But it is quite likely that his thoughts about women were entirely chaste, and his real sexual feelings still a source of embarrassment, which expressed itself in a show of giggly naïveté.

Win almost certainly misread erotic confusion as innocence. But John's presumed purity made his imminent entry into a pitiless war even more heartrending: the sacrifice of a boy before he has been able to become a man. In Japanese war propaganda, the sacrifice of young kamikaze pilots—most of whom were from the same social class as John—was pictured as something beautiful and pure: the fall of fresh cherry blossoms on the verge of full bloom. It is said that some Japanese mothers offered themselves to their sons before their last flight, so they no longer had to die as boys. Win would no doubt have been appalled by the very thought of such a thing, but her feelings as a prospective warrior's mother can have been no less fraught.

In February 1944, the invasion of Europe seemed a long way off. It "is still a matter of words," Win writes on February 10, and "we can't tackle the Japs until we eventually succeed in breaking the Germans . . . Poor old John. The news of the Japanese treatment of prisoners is not reassuring."

When Bernard hears about the Normandy landings on June 6, he is in Quetta, high up in the mountains of Baluchistan, near the borders of Iran and Afghanistan. These trips were not without their adventures. In Waziristan, a place now thick with the Taliban and other holy warriors, Bernard had to travel even then in a convoy of armoured cars to fend off hostile tribesmen. But listening to the news of D-Day on the radio in a remote hill station, surrounded by people who couldn't care less, makes him feel even more hopelessly stuck in the wrong place at the wrong time. On June 6, he writes, "So the greatest invasion of all time has begun. Good luck to all the chaps in it . . . How I wish I were back in Europe to lend a hand."

After listening to the radio, Bernard meets an old schoolmistress from Badminton, now teaching in Quetta, together with two of her female friends. They seem "much more interested in old school photos than the success or failure of an enterprise by which England stands or falls." All the more reason for Bernard to long to get back and experience "that top of the toes feeling" again, and rid himself "of the apathy that is bound up with so much in the East." He complains of getting fat around the waist, and is dying to have "a crack at the European front."

Such sentiments were stirred up by a combination of guilt, loneliness, boredom, and patriotism. I don't think Bernard had any romantic notions of being a hero. He thought typical war heroes were all a bit mad. Win reacted to his frustration in the way she always did when he suggested sleeping out on the frosty lawn at St. Mary Woodlands on Christmas Eve, except that in this instance the stakes were so much higher. She tried to talk him down.

June 18:

I want you back so much, and yet not on your conditions. Once more you seem determined to get into things up to the neck. From your veiled hints . . . I gather that you are agitating to join the invasion of France. You seem determined to plunge me from one anxiety into another. Don't you feel too, dearest, that to have perhaps a week or two at home, and then to be away again into the vortex with another heart-rending "goodbye" would only open up old wounds and upset the whole nervous system once more?

After the Allies have fought their way into France, Germany still has one more secret weapon. At the end of June 1944, Win and John spend a day in London. The atmosphere, she writes on June 29, was "distinctly unpleasant." The new German V-1 flying bombs ("doodlebugs") were "much worse than the 1940 Blitz." London was "almost empty, and the alert was on almost all day. Robots came over at intervals, flying low, and it is always a tense moment while you hear them roaring overhead & wait for the engine to switch off, followed by the crash."

Worse than the Blitz was an exaggeration, but this new jet-propelled weapon, also known as the "buzz bomb," would claim more than twenty-two thousand lives between June 1944 and March 1945.

Bernard is deeply concerned. He asks Win on July 27, 1944, "What is it that makes these bombs so devastating? Is it their persistence, their long & haphazard range or what?" The thought of the family being exposed to this new danger adds to his sense of helplessness and guilt. "Here am I in the army," he writes, "supposed to be taking part in a war, and I live in perfect safety, whereas you . . . I often feel quite ashamed of myself and I suppose it is partly this that unsettles me at times and urges me to fling myself into the scrum, if they would only let me."

They would not. And so Bernard had to follow what was going on in Europe from afar. On July 21, Win reports the excitement everyone is feeling about the failed German officers' plot against Hitler's life. The bomb put under the conference table at the Wolf's Lair, Hitler's East Prussian HQ, went off but didn't kill him. Instead, it left him with a hand permanently trembling behind his stooped back, and an even more paranoid disposition. The main plotters, mostly high-ranking aristocratic officers, were hanged on meathooks, "like cattle," in the führer's words. But Win rejoiced: "It shows the way the wind is blowing & may help to hasten the end." On the other hand, she writes, "I think it would be a pity if Hitler died a martyr's death before the end—it would be too easy for him."

Even if the Old Testament meant little to Win, she was no stranger to the feeling that an eye deserved an eye. But all in all, she concludes, in a burst of unusual perkiness, "things are looking up" and "perhaps after all it may not be too long now before we are all reunited for keeps & John released to pursue his studies." The garden in Mount Pleasant is looking its best, and "our sweet peas are marvellous this year."

Win's cheerfulness is matched by Bernard's answer, more than a month later, from a hospital on the North-West Frontier in what is now Pakistan. On August 28, he writes, "I say, what terrific news from everywhere in the West & what an extraordinary final chapter with all the rats leaving the sinking ship . . .

In the South of France it's all our honeymoon resorts—Arles,
Nimes . . . Do you remember those oysters on the way down
from Bordeaux?"

Of course, the moment of euphoria couldn't last. Less than
one month later, Field Marshal Bernard Montgomery decided
to drop a vast Allied army around the city of Arnhem in Holland to secure the bridges over the Rhine and get to Germany
ahead of his American rival, General George Patton. Casualties
in this disastrous enterprise exceeded fifteen thousand British,
Polish, Canadian, and U.S. soldiers. "Operation Market Garden" lasted for one week and ended on September 25. My
paternal grandparents, living in Nijmegen, were in the midst of
it, with bombs destroying the centre of their town and British
and Canadian troops putting up at their house.

Three days later Win writes a letter about seeing John off
for his army training as a combat engineer, or sapper: "We listened with bleeding hearts last night to this epic of Arnhem, &
from a few tentative questions, I realised that John had the
same thought as I had—Before not so very long he too might
be for it & the sappers have a slim chance. It looks now that we
cannot look for the end of this European business before the
Spring, & by that time John's year's training will be up & then
the fun in the Far East will begin in good earnest."

That John was as ill-suited to army life as he had been to a
spartan boarding school was clear to all. But there were other
problems, to do once again with the family background. Win
writes on October 6 that John is miserable in his "filthy camp"

near Liverpool, "and to add to his troubles, when on their second day there, the Padres came to talk to the lads, John and the
only other two Jews were ordered to return to their Barrack
Room as they were unable to provide Jewish services there.
Now John is not an Orthodox Jew in any case, & wouldn't understand a word of a Hebrew service, even if there were one;
on the other hand it would do him good to join in worship with
the others & perhaps gain the interest of one of the Padres. It
is the wretched Identity Disc that is the trouble. What ought he
to do about it?"

Win's worry is puzzling. It isn't clear whether John himself
shared it. Why would she, who never saw much point in religious worship, wish for her son to attend a Christian service?
And why was she so concerned about his identity disc? Would
she have preferred that he hide his background? According to
an often-repeated family story (I heard it as a child), John had
exclaimed to his army board, when asked about his religious
faith, "I'm a Jew and I'm proud of it." The same family legend
has it that Bernard and Win were both scandalized. The story
was usually told as a joke against them.

Perhaps they were scandalized. I can easily imagine Win
being opposed to John's rocking the boat in this manner. What
would those padres say? But there is no evidence of any of this
in the letters. In answer to Win's letter about John and the
padres, Bernard gives a perfectly reasonable account of his own
experiences in the army. "In both wars," he writes on October
22, "my true religion was in the unit records—the identity disc
was of small account. For the purposes of this war, with the
Nazi doctrine to combat in the event of capture I certainly

John (BOTTOM ROW, FAR RIGHT) in military training

wore a silver disc of my own with no mention of any religion . . .
The army deals with religions pretty broadmindedly, having
had years of experience with all the Indian races and customs.
There is never any objection raised for anyone to attend any
service outside his own creed . . . So I can't quite make out
John's trouble & I see no reason he shouldn't attend Padres
talks or services if he wants to."

I doubt that John was gripped by a strong desire to attend
any services, in either a synagogue or a church. He was never
religious. Especially in his American films, religion is usually
shown up as a grotesque trick perpetrated on gullible people. I
once asked him about this, not long before he died in
California. Yes, he answered, that is how he saw religion, as a
kind of hoax.

But that was America. He also had another view of religion.

You see it in his British films, like *Far from the Madding Crowd*, or *Yanks*, or, most poignantly, *Sunday Bloody Sunday*. Shared faith in these movies is more like a tradition, a form of cultural loyalty, which is the way many English people experience Anglicanism. In *Yanks* (1979), a middle-aged English lady, much like Win, left alone during the war by a husband in the army, is tempted to have an affair with a married American officer. They back off at the last moment from what might have turned into a sordid entanglement. When her husband returns in the end, we see them reunited in a country church, standing in the midst of the congregation, singing a hymn. Order has been restored. It is an order in which John felt no more at home than he did in the vast rootlessness of America, but I think he respected it.

Sunday Bloody Sunday was made in 1971. There is much of John in the main character, a gay Jewish doctor mixed up in a love triangle with a young artist and his female lover. Dr. Daniel Hirsh, played by Peter Finch, is comfortable in his skin, humorous, at ease with his homosexuality, and secular. He is also deeply attached to his family. That is the meaning of a long scene of his nephew's bar mitzvah. Hirsh remembers his own ritual coming-of-age. He takes part in the ceremony because he wants to be part of a tradition, even if he cannot quite believe in it.

In reality, neither John nor any of his nephews ever had a bar mitzvah (even though I did appear as an extra in the bar mitzvah scene). There was an element of play-acting in his religious experience. On the rare occasion that he would go to a synagogue, he would mumble the first few words of a prayer he barely knew, and then get lost in rhubarb. But he insisted on standing at an odd angle from the society he grew up in, unlike Win, hence the "I'm Jewish and I'm proud of it." Even though he could be as sentimental about Englishness— the country flowers, the ancient churches, the cornfields—as Bernard, he once told me he didn't regard the family as really being "English" at all. So what were they? I asked. "Well, not English."

What amazed me was to find a letter from Win, written on February 17, 1945, in which, far from expressing disapproval of John's claim to the military authorities, she actually admires him for it. John may be temperamentally unfit for soldiering, Win writes. Then follows one of her most moving statements: "I am glad to find that he has real moral courage. He told me that he was overjoyed that he had not changed his name, although he has sometimes been put through his paces on that account. He makes no bones about his race or German ancestry, although he has been baited a great deal—sometimes malevolently."

In spite of all the unfavourable comparisons Win has made between father and son, she finally salutes him for being braver than anyone else, braver than herself, braver even than Bernard.

Much of *Yanks* came from John's own wartime memories: the sex appeal of the American troops, their big ideas and easy manners, so different from cramped British attitudes. In the spring of 1944, more than one and a half million American troops were based in Britain, waiting for the invasion of Europe. They were, in the popular British phrase of the time, "oversexed, overpaid, and over here."

Win played concerts for the "Yanks" with the Finzi orchestra at a military base called Welford, a name I remember from country walks from St. Mary Woodlands. It is now a munitions depot just off the M4 motorway from London to Wales. Despite her warm feeling towards Americans in her Oxford days, Win's views of the Yanks during the war are not especially positive, but I think fairly typical of that time. As well as other things, the Americans posed an element of sexual danger, a bit like those Continental men whom Win saw on her trips to Italy as a young woman in 1924.

The following description of an encounter with American GIs, a year before D-Day, during an endlessly interrupted train journey from Paddington to Kintbury, sums up what many people probably felt, not just about American lecherousness, but American racism too.

July 11, 1943:

One or two American soldiers had been leering at me unpleasantly. Presently one, quite drunk, put his head through my window & started talking to me in a thick speech which I could hardly understand. I was very cold to him and sat tightly in my corner & then he grew maudlin, said he was from overseas & could he come in. Now I knew I had to keep my wits about me. From my scant experience of drunks, I knew you must never argue with them or let them suspect that you think they are

drunk, but just to talk to them kindly and patiently as
you would to a sick child. I talked & talked, anything to
keep him from pawing me, which he tried to do every
little while. He asked me if he might come and see me, &
I had to give him my address—anything to keep him
quiet . . . Inside me I was terrified, but I dared not show
it. He then got more and more vociferous on the subject
of the blacks, & a coloured American kept passing the
window, & knowing that they had all been drinking,
I was afraid that at any moment there would be an
unseemly brawl between them, & that I should have to
separate them. Shortly before the train left, to my great
relief, an English airman got in.

Bernard received this letter more than three months later in
the middle of October. "Your travelling experience," he writes
on October 19, "recounted with all its interesting details deserves a reply at some length & I shall shortly devote an air
mail letter to it & Americans in general."

Alas, that letter either got lost or was never written. I would
have liked to know more about Bernard's views on the Americans. From what little I was able to glean from his correspondence, he was better disposed to Britain's main allies than
Win, reflecting perhaps a greater distance from them.

Bernard's opinions on the Russian allies, too, are more in-
dulgent than Win's. In the autumn of 1943, he met a man on
the train "who knew Russia so well" and who claimed that the
Russians were reverting to their old imperial ways and had re-

cently kicked out all the Jews from important offices. "I wonder if that is the case," he writes. "I have often debated to myself & with others the relative merits or tyrannies of the Nazi and the Soviet dictatorships. We know so little about the latter but somehow one imagines that no nation could have fought a comeback so admirably unless the regime were pretty healthy."

Bernard was more inclined than Win to give the Soviet Union some benefit of the doubt. She was quicker to see the relative decline of British influence in the world, and deplored it. At the beginning of 1944, months before D-Day, she admits, on January 28, that "only the Russians seem able to deal successfully with the Boches, and that fact is rather bad for our prestige."

In November of that same year, after D-Day and the Battle of Arnhem, after the south of Holland has already been liberated, American troops are fighting inside Germany, and General Douglas MacArthur has landed in the Philippines, Win ends her letter on the fifth with this comment on the latest news: "The political future of the world looks bleak. Russia's attitude is quite blatant & uncompromising, & America self-seeking as ever, to say nothing of France or the lesser countries. Russia's attempts to corner all the European oil supplies strike me as ominous in the extreme. We really seem to be the only country seeking nothing for ourselves & dear, self-sacrificing Churchill globetrots to try and smooth out everybody else's troubles. But we shan't always have him. Worse luck. Goodnight beloved. Come soon to your adoring Win."

Churchill could do no wrong in Win's eyes, even when he

got hopelessly mixed up in the simmering civil war in Greece. The German occupation had inflamed old divisions between supporters of the pre-war fascist Greek government and its left-wing opponents even further. Left-wing guerrillas fought on the Allied side against the Germans and their Greek collaborators. At the end of the war, however, British troops were actually helping to crush a rebellion of left-wing guerrillas against a new Greek government that included former Nazi collaborators. The situation was murky. Communists dominated the Greek left. And yet many people in Britain felt that in this instance Winston was fighting on the wrong side. His rousing speech made in Athens on Christmas Day did nothing to stop Greece from spiralling into a horrendous civil conflict that would last until 1949.

But Win never doubted Churchill. On December 9, she writes, "I am feeling very angry about the mud which is being slung at Churchill by the leftwing extremists in our own country over this unhappy affair in Greece. Truly, he has courage and resilience beyond the ordinary or he would give up in despair & disgust. That section of the people and the press in the USA, who are always anxious to besmirch the British, have some good material to work on now, handed to them on a plate by our socialists."

Bernard replies on Boxing Day. He had spent his Christmas overeating in the officers' mess in Agra and playing games of squash to overcome the ill effects. Nights are spent in the open air despite the cold. He agrees with Win that the news "still remains tricky but slightly firmer and it's just like splendid Winston to go flying to Athens in an attempt to settle things on the spot."

Win tries to make Christmas at Kintbury "as happy an occasion as possible" in the absence of Bernard and John, who is finishing his training in the north of England. The remnants of the family join a group of carol singers in aid of new bells for the local church at Inkpen. Win tries to keep her "head high, but underneath there is a great ache & anxiety & weariness." An Algerian wine ("not bad when sufficiently warmed") is served with the Christmas turkey. Since this is a special occasion, Wendy is offered a cigarette by Win. "I believe," Win writes, "she smokes a lot in her digs at Lynmouth. They are growing up with a vengeance. Come back soon, for heaven's sake. We all miss you and need you so much."

The account of seventeen-year-old Wendy, described by Win as "a keen potential smoker," taking up a habit that would help to cut her life short less than three decades later, fills me with melancholy. I can still picture my mother, smiling through a grey haze of smoke from her Player's Navy Cut cigarettes. In fact, it was she who offered me my first smoke, as a kind of rite of passage, when I was about fifteen.

And so the last year of the war began, with a mixture of relief that surely now the end was in sight, and profound apprehension about horrors yet to come, not least to John. "Poor, poor John," Win writes on Christmas Eve. "Never was anyone less suited for the ordeal that is before him, and my heart bleeds for him, but fate moves on inexorably, & there is nothing I can do, except hope and pray."

Bernard responds to this on February 26, 1945, in a straight-forward manner that shows his deep humanity: "I know [John] is not a warrior, but then so few of us really are; only he worries about it more than most. We are nearly all cowards basically, or shall we say not cut out as heroes at any rate, but it is only the few unfortunates who are frightened that they will show up thus."

Nine

THE END

———.———

ear the end of April 1945, on the twenty-first to be exact, Bernard is on his way to Srinagar in Kashmir. News must have reached him of U.S. and British troops liberating the survivors in German concentration camps, Ohrdruf on April 4, Buchenwald on April 11, Bergen-Belsen on April 15—Auschwitz had already been reached by Soviet troops in January. The news provoked a rare outburst of fury in Bernard, who was normally so measured in his pronouncements, so keen to see the best in people and situations; if there was a silver lining anywhere, Bernard would be the first to spot it.

"The war," he writes, "is going stupendously, but what fiendish bastards the Bosch are, running true to their evil form right to the end with their atrocities. What is one to do with a nation like that, short of castrating the lot, which is obviously impossible, or is it?"

Three months earlier, on January 11, Bernard reacted rather

differently, and for that time with unusual human sympathy, to an encounter with soldiers from the other Axis power still at war: "I saw some Jap POW patients the other day at one hospital. Far from looking like the scowling villains depicted in the propaganda posters or the half-starved wretches written up in the papers, they looked rather a nice and cheery crowd who gave one a polite bow of the head as one passed through the ward. They made a much better impression than did those Germans of the Luftwaffe at Benenden in 1940. I was told these particular Japs were mostly farming people & no doubt longing to get back to their Mount Pleasants as the rest of us. How mad it all is."

But Japan was farther from home. And there was no silver lining in the German camps. The shock of seeing newsreels of filthy emaciated corpses stacked up in the woods of Belsen made many people in Britain feel the same way as Bernard about the Germans. General Eisenhower was so shaken by what he found at Ohrdruf in April that he wanted the whole world to know about it, in the hope (vain, as it turned out) that such things would never be possible again. (General Patton refused to see the corpses inside the torture chambers of Buchenwald, for fear that the sight would make him vomit.)

Apart from shared disgust, Bernard's letter, and Eisenhower's response to Nazi crimes, showed that the world was already moving on beyond the inevitable German defeat. People were looking ahead, imagining the future, beginning to draw lessons from the past, and starting to plan their post-war lives.

Bernard wonders whether his grown-up children will still

remember what he was like. He would have to get to know them all over again. He vows to stop seeking prestigious posts at London hospitals, for "those climbs up the ladder of ambition" only "led to frustration, disappointment & the wrong sort of hectic London life." And so, he writes, "I pray that this coming year will at length see the end of the world's travail, so that you and I, and others like us, together may again live in peace the rest of their years & try and make up for what we have lost." This was on January 11, 1945.

Win replies on February 7 that she cannot bear to wait much longer. Now that the reunion is in sight, she feels more anxious than ever: "I dream of you day and night, & curiously enough I even hark back to our childhood courtship and our feelings in those early days of 1914 when we first met. I feel that it will be almost the same all over again; in any case wildly thrilling."

Bernard thinks of John too. In the same letter where he vents his rage at the German fiends, he tries to be reassuring about the future of his eldest son, even though he could not have been more wrong in his prediction. "I am sorry for [John]," he writes. "He can't help his make up; still I think if he battles through the next few years satisfactorily & finally meets the right girl to love & help & advise him in life—like mine did & does—he should do alright."

Wendy, the other child who was so often the cause of parental concern—her untidiness, her sloth, her lack of scholarly application—had failed to get into Oxford. "She is such a dear," Win writes on September 13, 1944, "if only she were any

good at anything except being nice!" Bernard replies that being
nice "is already a rare achievement." BMB, the formidable
Badminton headmistress, had put Wendy's name in for a social
science course at the London School of Economics. Win does
not really approve: "I should have preferred King's or University College, if that had been possible, as the L.S.E. is full of
dagoes and Communists, but I suppose old Wendy will hold
her own."*

The term "cold war" was not heard of until October 1945,
when George Orwell used it in an essay about the atomic
bomb. As a description of Western relations with the Soviet
bloc it only entered the general lexicon in 1947, when the
American journalist Walter Lippmann wrote a book with that
title. If there were such a thing as a premature Cold Warrior,
Win was it. Her picture of the post-war future was darkly
clouded by the prospect of Communist villainy, near and far
from home.

Win's closest bugbears were her neighbours in Kintbury,
the Padels, who taught the youngest Schlesinger children before they were sent off to school. And then there were the refugee relatives in London, Maria and Ernst Stern ("the Stern
Gang"). On February 11, Win writes, "Maria is a complete
Red, à la Padel, influenced by her son David (née Hans), up
with the Russians & down with Churchill etc. The old, old slo-
gans that always make my blood boil."

"Uncle Joe" Stalin was still a hero to many people in En-

---

*I am not sure which "dagoes," or swarthy foreigners, Win had in mind. It is true
that the LSE was dominated by Harold Laski, a convinced Marxist, at the time.
His students had included Jawaharlal Nehru.

gland, including the much-revered BMB. And there were plenty of people who felt strongly that the world, and British society in particular, had to change. The old class privileges had become intolerable to men and women who had sacrificed so much in the war. Win was slower to spot this change in the national mood than Bernard, although she did make it clear that she had no intention of returning to the kind of social life they had had at Templewood Avenue. Those days are over, she writes on March 25: "I have strenuously avoided all artificial and polite social duties & functions which sap one's energy & waste valuable time to no purpose."

Win's conservatism had something to do with her pessimistic outlook. But her distrust of the Soviet Union, although often couched in exaggerated British patriotism, was not without foresight. She was frightened with good reason about the way the post-war world was shaping up. On April 28, she writes, "In certain quarters there is still a definite tendency to take rather than to give—and backed by the prestige of great strength and achievement, it looks as if there would be another dictatorship."

In May, Bernard alerts Win to an article he has read by a politician named Stephen King-Hall, on the situation in Russia. King-Hall reports that the "anti-God museums" have been closed down and Communism has been largely replaced by Russian nationalism. Attempts to evangelize the world with Communism have been abandoned. Bernard is impressed by this "unbiased account."

Win is not. She has read the article too, she writes on May 20, but still feels that the "present political unrest" in many parts of the world "is all at the instigation of Russia, whether

her game be Power Politics—with her as the Great Power—or world Communism. I am prepared to believe that the latter idea vanished with Trotsky, but that is not helping us any just now. If mankind continues grabbing by force & eschews sweet reason at the conference table, before the blood is dry upon the ground—shed so that reason might prevail—then it was shed in vain—and more will be shed within a generation."

"How can we ever deal with Stalin and his satellites," she continues, "shielded behind their obstinate secretive obscurity? It will be appeasement again, all along the line until the next war. Ghastly! We were born either too early or too late, but anyway into a terrible epoch. I have never been so deeply & depressingly affected by world events as I am now. That is why the victory over the Nazis has passed over me as though it had never been."

Win wrote this a year before Churchill's famous speech in Fulton, Missouri, about the Iron Curtain descending across the Continent, and three weeks after the German defeat, to which the Soviets had contributed so much. She had felt no better just before the Third Reich came crashing down.

The war had gone on for too long. Fear and separation from Bernard had taken their toll on Win. She didn't see, on April 28, how "the beastly Boche" could go on for much longer. And yet "curiously enough I can feel no elation or excitement about this approaching end—just a dull listlessness. When we invaded N. Africa and when Italy gave in, I was wild with excitement—now all that is over. I think we are all too tired."

In India, too, the writing was on the wall. Things could no

longer go back to the way they were, even if some people refused to admit it. After three years of working in military hospitals catering to Indian patients, mostly common soldiers
known as "sepoys," Bernard no longer spoke of the Indians as
children. To be sure, he still shared some of the common British views on the native populations. "Johnnie Gurkha" was "a
grand fellow, never depressed, always full of go." The Tibetans
in Sikkim were all "such nice friendly people and always meet
you on an equal footing." But he had more respect for the Indians than did many of his fellow countrymen.

On one of his forays out of Agra in February, Bernard
comes across a doctor who once had a flourishing practice in
Bombay and is now a major in the British army, "45," a refugee
from Germany, and a bit "too full of himself and his powers—a
common failing among this type & such a pity." Whether "this
type" refers to the German or the "45" provenance, or both,
Bernard doesn't say. At any rate, the major "does not much like
the idea of working under an Indian officer in command—
others, not ex-Germany, have I think tacitly felt the same. I
think it's nonsense and prejudice, but I haven't had the experience myself, so perhaps cannot judge."

On March 3, Bernard tells Win about a dinner he had had
with a padre with a sore eye, who had been in India for ten
years, and "I thought somewhat lost his sense of proportion as
a result. 'We were meant to rule, not serve under Indians' was
a sentiment that kept on cropping up on his part and yet he
thought he had, I suppose, a true Christian attitude to life."

There is no reason to think that Bernard was in favour of

Britain pulling out of India. He thought that British socialists, who were advocating such a course, were being naïve and misguided. My guess is that he envisioned a gradual process of handing more and more powers to the Indians until the British Raj became redundant, a process that could still take a long time. It was a common dream in the last stages of many empires, a harmonious confluence of Asians and Europeans who would produce the best of both worlds, a perfect merger of East and West. This notion was not limited to the European masters; some Asians, educated in Western schools and military academies, believed in it too. It was, as we now know, an illusion, not an ignoble one, but an impossible dream nonetheless.

Bernard gives a fine description of it, unwittingly, since he did not recognize it as an illusion, at least as far as the politics of the future were concerned. He is on his way by train to Benares on June 11, and two "grand fellows" join him in his compartment. They are a young British lieutenant colonel of an Indian regiment and his subedar major, the highest rank available to Indian officers. They had just come back from Rangoon. The Indian officer had served for thirty years in the British Indian forces and fought in both world wars. Bernard listens to the lieutenant colonel praising the prowess of the common Indian sepoy: "'Give us the specialists & ancillary services & the Indian army can beat the Jap hands down; we can do without your British line regiments,' he said."

Bernard's reaction, typically: "I was envious of the tales of their battles & felt acutely how much I belonged to the chair born division."

But at least he had had the satisfaction of a promotion in rank. On Win's letter of February 28, he is still addressed as colonel. On March 7, he is Brigadier B. E. Schlesinger. This, like so much else about Bernard, became something of a family joke. I was always told that it took him some time to come down to earth in post-war civilian life. On one occasion, taking a Sunday walk near Kintbury with his children, he was stopped by a local farmer who made it quite clear that they were trespassing on private land. "Don't you know who I am?" Bernard is supposed to have barked at the farmer. "Brigadier Schlesinger!" Whereupon the farmer replied, "I don't care if you're the king of England, you're still on my land."

In fact, the letters suggest that Win was far more excited about Bernard's promotion than he was. "My darling, august husband," she writes on March 7, "we are all thrilled at the news, and I shall be terribly proud of my Brigadier, when we sally forth together one of these days—<u>soon</u>." His reply, on March 20: "They just call it Brigadier, as far as I know—it's a sort of bastard rank, which only happens during a war. The next rank above is Major General."

Perhaps his modesty was feigned. But I don't think so. Being in the action, "having a crack" and all that, was what mattered to him far more than the pips on his uniform. Win took a slightly different view. Her cousin Ashley, now proudly serving in the British army too, had told her that Bernard would be entitled to wear his insignia as brigadier for sixty days after leaving India. "I <u>must</u> swank with my Brigadier, especially in the village," she writes on June 19.

———

And then it was all over.

"The great day has come," Win writes on May 7. "What a pity that you can't be here to celebrate the occasion with us." Wendy, Roger, and Hans were allowed to go to London for twenty-four hours to see the floodlighting of all the city's monuments that had survived the German bombs. They were there, in the Mall, in the midst of a delirious crowd facing Buckingham Palace, when the royal family and Churchill stepped onto the balcony. They cheered and sang and spent their pocket money on red, white, and blue favours and patriotic hats. They saw the three Lancaster bombers flying overhead dropping red and green flares and heard Churchill tell the nation to rejoice: "Advance, Britannia! Long live the cause of freedom! God save the King!"

Hilary wasn't with them, since the idea of her getting lost in "an excited, drunken crowd—especially Yanks" made Win "terribly nervous." Instead, on VE night Hilary and Susan joined the local crowd on Inkpen Beacon to help light one of the bonfires that stretched all the way to the Scottish Highlands, while church bells rang through the night. On the evening before, Roger and Wendy had climbed on the roof of Mount Pleasant to hoist the Union Jack, a large and imposing one that Win bought in Newbury for a large sum. Win writes, "I hope the Padels see it."

Of course, Win observes on May 10, it has been "a great deliverance, since that fateful May 10th, 1940, when all seemed lost. On that day, five years ago to-day, the man to whom we owe everything in this world, came into power . . . I have the greatest possible admiration for him & towards him I feel the deepest gratitude. I tremble lest he should now be supplanted in the pending General Election, he & all that he stands for."

"How marvellous it is to be British," she writes on May 18, after hearing Churchill speak on the radio, "what a grand, humane country this is. How quiet and modest & temperate are our leading men, in moments of direst peril or of most glorious triumph." Perhaps this was typical of the way many British people felt at the time, or these could have been the extravagant sentiments of the immigrants' child. All the same, VE Day came to Win as an anticlimax. She couldn't bring herself to join the revelries: "I missed you too much to celebrate at all, and so I improved the shining hour by doing a bit of extra work in the garden."

One week later, Win goes up to Manchester to see John. They stay at the Midland Hotel, a grand Edwardian Baroque establishment, which Hitler had earmarked as the Nazi Party HQ in occupied Britain. Perhaps some of the seedy atmosphere of the war years got lodged in John's memory and found a way into his film *Yanks*. The best scene in that movie is of the English wife, left behind on the home front, going off for what promises to be a weekend of sexual consummation with her friend, the lonely married American officer. They park in front of a large seaside hotel and see a young floozy emerge onto the balcony from one of the rooms to hang up her stockings on a line. Behind her hovers the shadow of a man in uniform. The shabbiness of it all prompts them to abandon their weekend escape.

Win on May 14:

> [John] is an awfully nice boy—really Parsifalian* &
> easily shocked, for all his apparent sophistication. He and
> I danced at the hotel on Saturday night—the first time I
> have danced since 1941 (Ireland) . . . The Midland Hotel
> is <u>wickedly</u> expensive & full of Yanks & their tawdry bits.
> Our chambermaid said she was really <u>grateful</u> to us for
> occupying three of her bedrooms over this week-end, as
> she is so appalled by what she generally gets—especially
> in the best double rooms with bathroom attached! One
> American girl went to bed drunk on Saturday night &
> demanded whiskey in her room in lieu of breakfast the
> next morning.

There is a prompt answer from Bernard on the twenty-ninth, which finally gets around to his promised thoughts about the Americans: "I can imagine the goings on of our Allies in the Midland Hotel. They are curious & without any subtlety or finesse (both wrong words, but you know what I mean) about women & only out for one thing & they are not very good at alcohol."

The announcement of VE Day came to Bernard when he was "slumbering off under my net in the grounds" of the Agra Barracks. It must have been a curious night, with some of his

---

*She means pure and naïve, like Wagner's hero.

fellow officers dancing around the mulberry bush—"my bed was the bush"—and sprinkling Bernard with drops of gin. Just as he was about to go to sleep again, he "received an S.O.S. in person" from an old patient "with a great psychological problem." The details of this problem are not divulged, but it kept Bernard up for half the night.

"My Beloved," Bernard writes on May 8. "On this historic day I must send you a word of love." He tells her not to fret "too much about world affairs & become too depressed. Anyway, you and I can't set them in order, and perhaps now after this war people will finally work out their salvation."

In Bernard, the German defeat sparked a bittersweet train of memory and reflection, which was more in his character than pessimism about the future. He thanks Win for taking care of "our protégées." "We can be pleased that in any case we have saved these twelve from the wreckage of Nazi clutches." He thinks about the horrors of the last six years, and "how senseless it all was." Now, he writes, "one can look back & remember what a near shave it all was & how in 1940/41 many of us wondered in our hearts really whether we should pull through, without letting on about this." He uses a word that would take on a more specific meaning much later: "So my darling, the longest & greatest Chapter One of the world's holocaust has ended."

About Chapter Two, the war in Asia, he is optimistic: "I don't think the Japanese war will take very long to finish. If Russia declares war, I believe the Japs will realise the wisdom of throwing in the sponge, or is it a towel, very soon. So possibly John may be spared much." The atomic bombs were still beyond imagination. But his prognosis was not wrong.

Bernard worshipped Winston Churchill no less than Win did. But he had a keener sense than she did that Churchill represented the past, which had been sweet to them in many ways, but to which it would be foolish to try to cling. There would be a general election in July, against the wishes of Churchill, who had wanted a coalition government to continue until Japan was defeated. The idea of the war hero being voted out of office made Win tremble. Bernard's feelings were more ambivalent. On May 27, he writes:

> I have mixed feelings about the election. England
> and the world still need the strong guiding hand of
> Churchill until the Jap is beaten & Europe settles
> into some sort of order. On the other hand, we must and
> can never slip back into our prewar ways, which nearly
> brought us to dissolution. The Conservatives have too
> many diehards, who correspond so closely to the
> old "ko hoi"* out here, and whose ideas are basically
> the same as in 1936–39. Moreover, if Labour got in
> there might be a better chance of good relations
> with Russia. On the other hand, Labour's expressed
> views on Indian affairs are so curious and unenlightened
> that I begin to wonder if the rest of their policy
> can be sound. I am in a muddle & so will stick to
> Churchill and all he stands for—he continues to be
> the soundest rock.

---

*Old colonials.

Bernard and Win had been luckier than most European Jews, lucky first of all that they were British, and thus stayed out of the Nazis' reach. Bernard pointed this out to Win in moments of despair, in January 1944, for example. Win had written on December 12, 1943, how she longed for his return, and how "our eternal wish is always next year, and next year . . . I mourn every day that I grow older without you." Bernard answers on January 1, 1944: "Dearest, I echo the same thoughts as you expressed in your last letter. I too feel that vital years for us are slipping by & now that I have nearly completed two years away, my restlessness is sometimes difficult to keep in bounds . . . If only I could see you for a month or so . . . But it just can't be & then I tell myself that thousands are in a much more parlous state than we are, with hope and everything gone, their lives ruined, everything they have built up shattered."

He was right, of course, even though the number of close relatives who had perished was not as high as it might have been. Many had managed to get out of Germany in time. Some who failed to do so had been extraordinarily lucky. Hugo Natt and his wife, Clara, who had fled to London, had given up their son, Bernard, as lost, after he had been taken to a concentration camp in Belgium. Win writes on June 20 that a cable had just been received from him, saying, "Leaving Czechoslovakia for Holland." He had presumably survived in Theresienstadt, a camp for relatively privileged prisoners, many of whom were later transported to Auschwitz, if they had managed to withstand starvation, illness, and abuse. However, Win continues, there was "no word of the Schusters. I am afraid they are all lost."

They were indeed all murdered, after they had been picked up by the Nazis in Holland, one by one, leaving in an extra twist of cruelty the severely handicapped Martin till last.

In the case of some Jewish families, the collective experience of Nazi persecution and murder had created a stronger sense of common identity. While it is true that the Jewish catastrophe was often talked about at family gatherings, Win's feelings were as ambivalent as they always had been. This was not really a question of suppression or denial. What it meant was that she remained true to her background and class.

Here she is, on March 9, 1945, meeting Vera Baer for lunch in London. Vera was one of the hostel children, the one whose photograph Win had admired because there wasn't "a trace of 45." Win declares that she is "quite a pleasant looking girl, rather short and thickset, but still quite fair. While we were at lunch, her mother suddenly turned up—quite unbidden—but with the typical cheek of her race and type . . . She looked a typical East Ender, dark & sallow, with a bright handkerchief tied round her head & carrying a large basket full of 'Delikatessen.' She is cook to some people called Taylor (née Schneidermacher). Vera talks perfect English & carries a definite veneer of a good boarding school education."

Like Hans Levy, Vera had made a successful transformation in Win's eyes. Hans had even taken an interest in cricket. "By Jove," Win writes on June 23, "how he had profited by living in England in a wholly English community."

Another one of the protégées, Marianne Mamlok, had decided to go a step further and become a Christian. This was a
tricky issue among children of the *Kindertransport.* Some had
been taken in by Christian families, who then tried to convert
them. Some had taken this step themselves. Marianne had evidently wanted to convert, and Win had swiftly given her con-
sent. The child had lost both her parents, and Win felt it would
do her good to join a religious community of her choice. However, no sooner had she done this than "an indignant letter"
was received "from one—Rabbi Levine," who had threatened
to ensure that the child would no longer get any support from
the Jewish refugee organization, Bloomsbury House, if she
went through with it. Win writes on July 2, "Everyone is agreed
that it is a deplorable letter & will go far to increase anti-
Semitism—& with justice."

Bernard answers on the eleventh: "I am sorry about the
Marianne bother. How narrow-minded people are. What the
hell does it matter, provided you do your stuff & the conversion from one to another has been carefully thought-over & is
not just a flash in the pan. Of course, we'll see her along."

This reaction was typically generous. Neither Bernard nor
Win felt that conversion was a betrayal of the tribe; Win was
certainly more tolerant of this move than she was of German
accents or "typically East End" behaviour. But things are always a little different when one's own children are involved.
Hilary had always been searching for spiritual solace of one
kind or another, unlike her brothers and sisters, who had never
shown any interest in religious faith. When I grew up, Wendy
was happy to talk about many aspects of being "45," but never

about the religion itself, about which she was wholly ignorant. But Hilary was a seeker from the beginning.

In June 1945, while still at Badminton School, Hilary had written to Win about her religious feelings and her desire to become a Christian. Win's reaction was deeply sceptical, as though Marianne Mamlok had been forgotten. She writes to Bernard, on June 5, "I have told her that it would require years of mature thought and study of the subject before she could be entitled to take such a step, and that now there are more opportunities in the holidays for attending services at the LJS [Liberal Jewish Synagogue], she should give that a chance."

Bernard answers on June 13: "I think your first reaction to Hilary's religious wonderings was correct. She must think it well over but I should be the last to stand in the way of a conversion through true conviction. At present I think she is too young for a final decision."

She was in fact no younger than Marianne Mamlok. But her conviction must have been firm, for after a long peregrination via a Presbyterian in Switzerland and various evangelists in South America, she ended up in the Catholic Church as a member of the Opus Dei. Marianne not only became a Christian, as she had wished, but lost her way in a disastrous marriage with a German former Nazi.

Even though I must confess to having a slight prejudice against conversions, I don't mean to cite these examples as a warning against them. But then I don't have any faith to convert from. Perhaps Hilary and Marianne did not either. With all their doubts and contradictions, Bernard and Win hung on to what they always were, liberal Jews whose national loyalties were never allowed to conflict with what was left of their tribal, or ethnic, or official religious identification. As is clear from Bernard's letters, he was happy to find spiritual comfort wherever he could. And both found the deepest expression of their feelings in music. But what they clung to more than ever as the war was nearing its end was their English idyll, expressed in her passion for gardening, his dreaming over *Country Life*, her faith in English boarding schools, his in fresh air and exercise, and their celebration of the Berkshire countryside. That, perhaps, was their truest "religion."

While waiting for Bernard finally to be released from the army, Win kept returning to their idyll in her last letters of the war. This is how she ended her letter on June 23: "Goodnight my beloved. It is a glorious sunny evening, & Berkshire & our particular garden are looking lovely, I wish we could walk down hand-in-hand to shut up the news & admire the view on the way, & rejoice in each other's proximity."

Of course, they never could shut up the news, and Bernard did not give up his medical ambitions in London, and they didn't run a farm together, as Win had wished in one of her last letters, and Bernard continued to demonstrate his patriotism by volunteering for army duty every time there was a crisis, well beyond the age that his services were required. But the idyll lived on, as their mutual dream of a safe haven.

Win desperately hoped that Bernard could be home by July 21, to hear my mother, Wendy, and her sister Hilary sing in their school production of Gilbert and Sullivan's *HMS Pinafore,* the comic opera about the love of a captain's daughter and a common sailor that makes fun of the absurdities of excessive patriotism.

I have in my hand a telegram stamped by the Newbury post office on July 13, 1945. It is addressed to "Schlesinger—Mount Pleasant Kintbury." It reads: "Flying home. Should make the meeting twenty first. So Thrilled. Bun Schlesinger."

EPITAPH

—·—

Bernard and Win are buried in Willesden, in north-west London. The United Synagogue Cemetery is divided by a wall of plain sandy-coloured brick, of the kind that was used in many late Victorian terraced houses. On one side of the wall are the graves of Orthodox Jews, including Bernard's parents. Liberal Jews are buried on the other side. The two sides are invisible to each other.

It is not easy to find their graves if you don't know where to look. They are not marked by slabs of marble or ostentatious tombs. All there is, half hidden under a small bed of roses, near a sculpture of a weeping woman and the wall that divides the Orthodox from the Liberals, is a small white tablet with the names and dates of Bernard E. Schlesinger, Winifred H. Schlesinger, and John R. Schlesinger.

None of them had an easy ending. Bernard was the first to go, in 1984. His mind had begun to wander some years before.

In the garden of their last home
at Boxford, Berkshire

Win could no longer talk to him in the way she had for almost seventy years, about politics, the news, the family, friends, music. I was living in Hong Kong at the time. Even in his diminished mental state, Bernard still kept up his habit of writing letters. In his last letter to me, he confused me with my cousin Paul. But to the very end of his life, he never forgot to thank Win for being his wife.

Left alone, physically frail, in constant pain, and humiliated by her dependence on others, but mentally as sharp as ever, Win had a miserable two years before she followed Bernard. And John, felled by two strokes, was first reduced to a shadow of his former self, wheeled around the cacti in his garden at Palm Springs, California, giving directions as though on a ghostly movie set, and then lost the capacity to communicate anything at all.

I walked from Willesden tube station to the cemetery on a windy late-summer day. Greasy paper bags and plastic containers were blowing across the streets. Willesden is not the most attractive part of London. Largely rural until the nineteenth century, it was once a place of pilgrimage: a sacred well with healing properties was located there, as was a statue of the Black Madonna, which was burnt along with other popish images when the Catholic Church came under attack in the sixteenth century. From the late 1930s, many Jewish refugees from Germany and Eastern Europe moved to Willesden, by then a largely working-class area.

Much has changed in London since then. Willesden has now become one of the most mixed immigrant districts in London, with Iranian supermarkets, Polish groceries, Iraqi bakeries, Hindu temples, Islamic colleges, Chinese hairdressers, halal butchers, Turkish kebab shops, and Pakistani cab companies. It is no longer the England that Bernard and Win knew. Their rural idyll of Berkshire seems very far from there. Even the genteel streets of Hampstead, where they grew up, feel distant, even though Fitzjohn's Avenue and Parsifal Road are only a few miles away.

Thinking about my grandparents, and my uncle John, as I

stand over the wilting roses that cover their names, I feel the strong sense of regret that I always have when I think of people I loved who are no longer alive, regret that they don't know me now, instead of my younger self, with all the clumsiness that goes with youth. I think of all the silly things I have uttered, every awkward move to impress, all the preening and posing, and wince. But this has less to do with my grandparents or my uncle than with the passing of time. One's younger self always looks embarrassing in hindsight. I wonder if they would have thought so, if they had reread the letters they wrote in their teens, twenties, or even later. If so, I hope they would have forgiven me for making them public.

Epitaphs are chosen either by people before they die or by others who loved them. There are no epitaphs on the plaque that marks the graves of Bernard and Win. At her funeral in Oxford, in 1986, Rabbi Rayner of the Liberal Jewish Synagogue in St. John's Wood called Win a *Tzaddeket*, the Hebrew word for a righteous woman. I doubt whether she would have recognized the word, but it seems apt.

At Bernard's memorial in London, in 1984, John read a poem by e. e. cummings, titled "My Father":

> his flesh was flesh his blood was blood:
> no hungry man but wished him food;
> no cripple wouldn't creep one mile
> uphill to only see him smile.

This seems apt as well. But one of Bernard's letters to Win might be his most fitting epitaph. It was written on December

2, 1941, five days before the Japanese bombed Pearl Harbor. The letter was sent from Bangor, Northern Ireland. Bernard expresses the hope that one day soon they will be reunited and "this time for good in a better world." Then he goes on to say, "Recently I have come to disbelieve in any Heaven or Hell. My idea is that our hereafter, good or bad, is the memory of ourselves we leave behind."

By memory I don't think he meant norms of behaviour or morality, or worldly success, that following generations should emulate. If that is what he meant, he might have been disappointed. As in most families, the lives of his children and grandchildren are riddled with common human failures. Bernard and Win's marriage set an almost impossible standard.

But Bernard was anything but an arrogant man. What he meant, I think, is that he made the best he could out of his life, and hoped that the best would live on in the memories of his offspring. The desire to live up to this memory, to seek the approval of the dead, much as one did when they were still living, is both a curse and a blessing. It is a curse because it is an unattainable goal, and a blessing because it inspires us to do better.

The choices made by Bernard and Win, the stories they told themselves, are not mine, but they have affected my choices, for good and for ill. It is in the nature of eulogies and memorials that the dead are idealized. This book about their correspondence is not a eulogy. That Bernard and Win had their flaws might have been apparent. I loved them not despite their flaws, but also because of them; they too live on in my own.

I do not expect the reader of their letters to love them as I did. But I hope to have honoured their memories. This is my way of placing a stone on their graves, sprinkling the English roses that mark their ashes, and tending to their afterlife. It would be good to end this book in the way of a film, with a dolly shot moving away from the tablet that bears their names, the scene fading to the rolling credits of all the people touched by their lives.

But for me, I know that the movie will never quite end. And as long as there are readers, the hereafter of Bernard and Win is assured by the written testimony they left behind.

Acknowledgements

I would like to thank my sister, Ann Buruma, for her enormous help in tracking down letters, photographs, and other bits of information. Writing about intimate family relations is always a tricky business. I am deeply grateful for the generous spirit in which Richard Levy and Hilary Schlesinger read the manuscript, which not only saved me from errors—they were *there*, after all, I was not—but improved the book. Michael Raeburn kindly allowed me to read some of his father's letters. Lilli Zimet shared her memories with me. And without the loyal readership and encouragement of Eri Hotta, my wife, and Isabel Buruma, my daughter, I would have found it much harder to soldier on.

I owe a debt to Jin Auh and Jacqueline Ko of the Wylie Agency for their unstinting support. And to Scott Moyers and Mally Anderson, my fine editors at Penguin Press, whose skill and dedication to the written word are all too rare, even among professionals.

Index

A Note About the Author

Ian Buruma was educated in Holland and Japan. He has spent many years in Asia, which he has written about in *A Japanese Mirror* and *Bad Elements*. His other books include: *The Wages of Guilt*, *Anglomania* and *Year Zero*. Buruma lives in New York, where he teaches at Bard College. He writes frequently for *The New York Review of Books*, *The New Yorker*, and many other publications in the US and Europe.